中国思想文化术语多语种对外翻译
标准化建设项目成果
CHINESE THINKING AND CULTURE
MULTILINGUAL TERMINOLOGY DATABASE

中华源·河南故事
CHINESE CIVILIZATION
Stories from Henan

丝绸之路
THE SILK ROAD

主编 梁留科
EDITOR-IN-CHIEF: LIANG LIUKE

河南大学出版社
HENAN UNIVERSITY PRESS
·郑州·

图书在版编目（CIP）数据

中华源·河南故事. 丝绸之路 / 梁留科主编. -- 郑州：河南大学出版社，2019.3（2021.12重印）
　ISBN 978-7-5649-2473-7

Ⅰ.①中　Ⅱ.①梁　Ⅲ.①地方文化—河南—通俗读物②丝绸之路—通俗读物　Ⅳ.①G127.61-49②K928.6-49

中国版本图书馆CIP数据核字(2019)第047030号

责任编辑	侯若愚
责任校对	毛晓旭
封面设计	翟淼淼
出版发行	河南大学出版社
	地址：郑州市郑东新区商务外环中华大厦2401号　邮编：450046
	电话：0371-86059701（营销部）0371-86059753（大众读物分公司）
	网址：hupress.henu.edu.cn
排　版	河南博雅彩印有限公司
印　刷	河南博雅彩印有限公司
版　次	2020年1月第1版
印　次	2021年12月第2次印刷
开　本	710 mm×1010 mm　1/16
印　张	10
字　数	140千
定　价	57.00元

版权所有　侵权必究
本书如有印装质量问题，请与河南大学出版社营销部联系调换。

"中华源·河南故事"系列丛书编委会

顾　　问　　黄友义　杨　平　范大祺
名誉主任　　穆为民　何金平
主　　任　　付　静
副 主 任　　陈志伟　刁玉华　李向前　李　镇　梁留科
　　　　　　刘金锋　孔留安　史永庆　许二平　万正峰
　　　　　　杨建伟　杨玮斌　王建修　王自文　张改平
　　　　　　张松文　赵卫东

主　　编　　付　静
执行主编　　杨玮斌
编　　委　　陈　玮　丁　锐　高　阳　徐恒振

中华源·河南故事·丝绸之路

主　　编　　梁留科
副 主 编　　陆志国　梅中伟（英文）
中文撰稿　　郑　学　毛阳光　赵豫云　伍纯初
英文译者　　步国峥　丁　政　杨　燕　郝璐璐
英文审校　　〔英〕Craig Hunter

The Editorial Committee
Chinese Civilization
Stories from Henan

Consultants	Huang Youyi Yang Ping Fan Daqi
Honorary Directors	Mu Weimin He Jinping
Director	Fu Jing
Deputy Directors	Chen Zhiwei Diao Yuhua Li Xiangqian Li Zhen
	Liang Liuke Liu Jinfeng Kong Liu'an Shi Yongqing
	Xu Erping Wan Zhengfeng Yang Jianwei
	Yang Weibin Wang Jianxiu Wang Ziwen
	Zhang Gaiping Zhang Songwen Zhao Weidong

Chief Editor	Fu Jing
Executive Chief Editor	Yang Weibin
Editors	Chen Wei Ding Rui Gao Yang Xu Hengzhen

Chinese Civilization
Stories from Henan
The Silk Road

Editor-in-Chief	Liang Liuke
Associate Editors-in-Chief	Lu Zhiguo Mei Zhongwei (English Text)
Writers	Zheng Xue Mao Yangguang Zhao Yuyun
	Wu Chunchu
Translators	Bu Guozheng Ding Zheng Yang Yan
	Hao Lulu
Translation Proofreader	Craig Hunter (U.K.)

总　序

中国是世界四大文明古国之一，也是世界上唯一的古代文明传统未曾中断的国家。河南省地处中国中东部，是中华文明和中华民族的重要发祥地，在中国五千年的文明史上，河南作为国家政治、经济、文化的中心就长达三千多年。从某种意义上讲，一部河南史就是半部中国史。这里是中华人文始祖黄帝的故乡，是古丝绸之路的东方起点，是少林功夫和陈氏太极的发源地，这里创建了中国历史上最早的都城，镌刻了中国最古老的文字，诞生了中国最初的商业文明。

伴随着新时代的荣光，河南经济社会发展迅速，人民生活水平显著提升，这是自力更生、艰苦奋斗的历史结果，也是对外开放带来的益处。河南经济社会的发展、人民生活方式的改变都植根于深层次的文化积淀。为了让世界更多地了解河南，让河南更好地走向世界，2018年以来，河南省外事办认真研析了这片古老土地上的历史文化资源和时代风貌，组织各领域权威专家学者，编译了"中华源·河南故事"中外文系列丛书，选取少林功夫、太极拳、中医、汉字、文物、焦裕禄、红旗渠、丝绸之路、古都、农业、手工艺等多个主题，力图以故事的方式向世界展现一个立体、全面、真实的河南。

当今世界，人类文明无论在物质还是精神方面都取得了巨大进步，特别是物质的极大丰富是古代世界完全不能想象的。同时，当代人类也面临着许多突出的难题，比如，贫富差距持续扩大，物欲追求奢华无度，个人主义恶性膨胀，社会诚信不断消减，伦理道德每况愈下，人与自然关系日趋紧张，等等。要解决这些难题，不仅需要运用人类今天发现和发展的智慧和力量，而且需要运用人类历史上积累和储存的智慧和力量。河南历史文化底蕴深厚、包容性强，在今天仍极具现实意义。中原文化蕴含的思想智慧有助于修身养性，推动人类社会进步发展，焦裕禄精神、红旗渠精神所体现的为民爱民、艰苦奋斗的价值取向是构建人类命运共同体的力量源泉。我们期待与读者们一起从河南故事中汲取更多的智慧和力量，共同创造更加美好的未来。

Series Foreword

China is one of the four ancient civilizations in the world, and is also the only country in the world where the ancient civilization has not been interrupted. Located in east-central China, Henan province is an important cradle for the Chinese nation and the Chinese civilization. In the course of the five thousand years of Chinese history, for more than three thousand years it served as the political, economic and cultural center of the country and therefore, as generally accepted, represents half of the history of China. Henan is the native place of Yellow Emperor, the cradle of Chinese culture, the starting point of the ancient Silk Road in the east, and the birthplace of Shaolin Kungfu and Chen-style Taijiquan—typical examples of the world-renowned Chinese martial arts. It was here that the earliest capital city in China was founded, the oldest Chinese characters engraved, and the earliest commerce took shape.

In the new era, Henan has witnessed rapid growth in its economy and remarkable improvement of people's living conditions, owing to the national reform and opening-up policy and unremitting endeavoring of the people. Modern economic achievements and social development as well as the changes of way of life could be traced back to its traditional values and cultural heritages. To enable people from other countries to understand Henan, and let the province integrate more efficiently into the world development, the Foreign Affairs Office of the People's Government of Henan province, has organized teams of authoritative experts and scholars in relevant fields to compile this *Chinese Civilization: Stories from Henan* in Chinese and other foreign languages since 2018, by crystallizing the excellence of traditions and outstanding features of modern development. The book series include *Shaolin Kungfu, Taijiquan, Traditional Chinese Medicine, Chinese Characters, Cultural Heritage, A Model Official — Jiao Yulu, Man-made River — Hongqiqu Canal, the Silk*

Road, *Ancient Chinese Capitals*, *Handicraft* and *Feeding the People — Agriculture*, etc, attempting to present a panoramic picture of the province.

In today's world, human civilization has made great progress in both material accumulation and cultural and ethical advancement, and the great abundance of materials today, especially, is beyond the imagination of the ancient people. At the same time, however, modern people are also confronted with a lot of problems, such as the widening gap between the rich and the poor, the indulgence in pursuit of luxury and extravagance, the undesirable extension of individualism, the decline of social integrity, and the increasing tension between man and nature. To solve these problems, we need to draw on the wisdom and powers developed today as well as those accumulated in the past. Henan is endowed with a rich historical and cultural heritage characterized by its inclusiveness, and such a heritage remains significant today. The intelligence and wisdom in Henan culture are conducive to self-cultivation and to the promotion of social development. The spirit of serving the people and relentless struggle, as embodied in *Jiao Yulu* and *Hongqiqu Canal*, provides source of strength for building a community with a shared future for mankind. It is our hope that, wisdom and strength from Henan stories, could lead us to a shared brilliant future.

前　言

丝绸之路是一条古老的商业贸易之路，是一条连接东西方的文化之路，其起源于公元前138年张骞出使西域，以输出中国最重要的贸易商品"丝绸"而得名。19世纪末，德国地理学家李希霍芬提出丝绸之路的概念，指出丝绸之路是"从公元前114年至公元127年，中国与中亚、中国与印度间以丝绸贸易为媒介的西域交通道路"，这里重点说明的是丝绸之路的商业性质。其实，汉代以后，丝绸之路被诸多朝代所经营，尤以唐代为盛，它连接了世界四大文明古国、世界三大宗教，突破了商业范畴，是一条不折不扣的文化交流之路。

河南是中华民族与中华文明的主要发祥地之一，同时也是中国古代四大发明的主要发明地。在古代重要的都城中，河南占有重要的位置，洛阳、郑州、开封、安阳、商丘、许昌等都是著名的古都，历经大小三十余个朝代，其中，洛阳素有十三朝古都的美誉。北宋著名政治家司马光曾感慨道："若问古今兴废事，请君只看洛阳城。"这说明了洛阳在中国历史上的显著地位。现代学者也普遍认同"一部河南史，半部中国史"的说法，古代河南曲折发展的轨迹是中华民族命运跌宕起伏的缩影。河南又是中国姓氏文化与人口迁徙的重要起源地，故有"豫见中国，老家河南"之说。

河南具有优越的地理位置，这里既有古老厚重的文化底蕴，又充满了多元交融的文化气息，是东西方文化交流的重要枢纽，在丝绸之路发展史上发挥了不可替代的作用。河南独特的位置与历史文化决定了其丝绸之路重要节点的地位，这里是神秘宗教文化的传播地，酣畅浑厚的诗歌在这里涌动，瓷器、茶叶、丝织品穿梭于古道上，医药、天文学等也实现了穿越时空的碰撞、打破地域的对话。丝绸之路，扮演着民族融合、域域合作的重要媒介，是诉说古老中国故事的文化线。

千年的驼铃从历史的深处响起，化作点点的星光点缀在这古老的丝绸之路上。这是铿锵的前进的声音，我们在交流中共同进步，在互通中一起繁荣，自古皆然；这同样是飞翔的声音，新时代，新未来，如今"一带一路"倡议让这条古老的道路再次焕发生机，未来可期。

你我同住地球村。文明互鉴，有容乃大。古路新通衢，天下皆朋友。这是新起点，让历史走进现在；这是新发展，让河南联通世界。万物互联，商贸往来从此再扬帆；常来常往，文明交流从此再出发。

Preface

The Silk Road, featured by commercial trade and cultural communication, dates back to 138 B.C. when Zhang Qian (a Chinese official who served as an imperial envoy in the late 2nd century B.C. during the Han Dynasty) was dispatched to the Western Regions (referring to west of Yumen Pass, most often Central Asia). It derives its name from the silk trade along the route. At the end of 19th century, the term "Silk Road" was coined by Ferdinand von Richthofen, a German geographer, who reckoned that it serves as a route for silk trade connecting China, Central Asia and India from 114 B.C. to 127 A.D. His remark highlighted the commercial function of the Silk Road. Actually, the Silk Road had been run by several dynasties since the Han Dynasty (206 B.C. – 220 A.D.) and saw its prosperity in the Tang Dynasty (618 A.D. – 907 A.D.). It definitely enhances cultural interaction beyond commercial trade, for it connects the world's four great civilizations (ancient Babylon, ancient Egypt, ancient India and ancient China) and three major religions (Christianity, Islam and Buddhism).

As a birthplace of Chinese people and civilization, Henan Province is home to four great inventions of ancient China. It boasts such well-known ancient capitals as cities of Luoyang, Zhengzhou, Kaifang, Anyang, Shangqiu and Xuchang, and thirty-plus dynasties established their capitals in these cities. Among them, thirteen dynasties established their capitals in Luoyang. "The ebb and flow of ancient China could be well represented in Luoyang," exclaimed Sima Guang, a prominent statesman of the Northern Song Dynasty (960 A.D. – 1127 A.D.). This manifests the vital role Luoyang played in the history of China. Additionally, it is widely recognized in modern times that half of Chinese history can be told by Henan Province as the ups and downs of Henan Province epitomizes that of China. Meanwhile, a saying goes that most of Chinese can find their ancestry in Henan Province since it is where

China's surname culture and population immigration originate from.

Endowed with convenient geographical location and profound and diverse culture, Henan Province is also indispensable to the Silk Road as a hub of communication between eastern and western culture, where mysterious religious culture spreads, powerfully emotive poetry thrives, trade in porcelain, tea and silk fabrics booms, and traditional Chinese medicine and astronomy communicate. Apart from boosting ethnic unity and regional cooperation, the Silk Road is a carrier to make people know more about the ancient Chinese culture.

Thousands of years of camel bells resound from the depths of history, turning themselves into stars dotted on the ancient Silk Road. This is the sonorous voice of common progress and prosperity through mutual exchanges since ancient times. This is also the sound of take-off. In such a new era, the Belt and Road Initiative makes this ancient road revitalized again with bright future.

We live in the global village. It is also really a big family with inclusiveness and mutual learning from civilizations. From this ancient road, and now a new thoroughfare, come friends all over the world. This is a new starting point, the old history has been melting into the present; this is new development, Henan has been connecting the world. More exchanges, more opportunities. With this common ground, we together step into tomorrow hand by hand, shoulder by shoulder.

目 录   Contents

第一章 一条古道与一片热土 ... 001
    一、繁荣的丝绸之路贸易 ... 004
    二、繁华的丝绸之路城市 ... 012
    三、发达的丝绸之路交通 ... 024
    四、联通世界的"一带一路" ... 036

Chapter I An Ancient Road and a Thriving Land ... 001
    I. Prosperity of the Silk Road Trade ... 005
    II. The Prosperous Silk Road Cities ... 011
    III. Advanced Silk Road Transportation ... 023
    IV. The Belt and Road Connecting the World ... 037

第二章 物质交流与技术扩散 ... 043
    一、丝绸的生产和外销 ... 044
    二、贵重商品的输入 ... 050
    三、生物品种的交流 ... 062
    四、医药、天文历法的交流 ... 068

Chapter II The Exchange of Goods and Technologies ... 043
    I. Silk Production and Export ... 045
    II. Introduction of Valuable Commodities ... 053
    III. Communication of Biological Species ... 063
    IV. The Exchange of Medical Technology, Pharmacy, Astronomy and Calendars ... 069

第三章　思想交流与文化传播　　　　　　　　　　079
　　一、宗教的传入与演化　　　　　　　　　　　080
　　二、美术的东传与西渐　　　　　　　　　　　094
　　三、音乐、文学的交流与传播　　　　　　　　122

Chapter III Ideological Exchange and Cultural Communication　079
　　I. Introduction and Evolution of Religions　　081
　　II. The Spread of Art from East to West　　　095
　　III. Music and Literature Exchanges　　　　　119

附录　中国历史年代简表　　　　　　　　　　　　144
Appendix　A Brief Chronology of Chinese History　144

第一章

一条古道与一片热土

Chapter I

An Ancient Road and a Thriving Land

从意大利罗马到中国河南,现代人乘坐飞机大约需要飞行十八个小时。如果古罗马的恺撒大帝想要进行同样的旅行,他需要花费多长时间?这个问题当然没有答案,但它并不荒谬,因为在恺撒生活的时代已有一条交通线路连接起这两个遥远的地区。

河南是中华文明的核心地区和发源地,最初意义上的"中国"就在这里诞生。中国现存古老的传世文献《尚书》把"中国"理解为河南及其周边的黄河中游地区。何尊(图1-1),西周初期青铜器,1963年出土,中国首批禁止出国(境)展览的64件文物之一。尊内底部铸有122字铭文,记载周武王灭商以后,周人建设王都洛邑的历史,其内容可与传世文献《尚书·周书·多方》相印证。铭文中有"宅兹中国(定居在这中央之国)"一句,这是"中国"一词最早的文字记载,意指以河南西部洛阳盆地为中心的中原地区。从西周营建东都洛邑算起,此后两千余年的时间里,有十余个统一或者割据政权在此建都。在这片沃土之上,有中国最早的都邑、最丰富的古代遗迹和最精彩的英雄传奇。

河南也是东西方文化汇合、交流的集散地。一条古老的商路由此出发,

图1-1 何尊

Fig.1–1 He Zun (an ancient wine vessel)

From Rome in Italy to Henan Province in China, it takes modern people eighteen hours to fly by air. How long would it take Julius Caesar to travel the same way in ancient times? Obviously, there is no practical answer to this question, which, however, is not a ridiculous one. In the times of Caesar there was a passage between these two regions so distant from one another.

Henan is the kernel and cradle of Chinese civilization. The literal meaning of China's Chinese name, the central land, originated here. *Shangshu* (also translated as *The Book of Documents,* a collection of publicized imperial documents), the oldest Chinese surviving documents, interpret "the central land" as the middle reaches of the Yellow River in Henan and its surrounding areas. He Zun(fig.1−1), a piece of bronzeware made during the early Western Zhou Dynasty, was unearthed in 1963, and it was listed in the first national project of prohibiting a batch of 64 cultural antiques from overseas exhibition. The base of He Zun bears a 122-character inscription, which records the history of the Zhou people building the capital of Luoyi after the cessation of the Shang Dynasty, which was conquered by King Wu. Its contents can be corroborated with a document entitled *Duofang* in *Zhoushu* (documents of the Zhou Dynasty) chapter of *Shangshu*. The inscription contains the phrase "settled in the central country", the earliest literary record of the phrase "central country", which refers to the Central Plains region centered around the Luoyang Basin in the western Henan area. Since the foundation of Luoyi, the eastern capital of the Western Zhou Dynasty, more than ten unified or separated dynasties established their capitals here during more than 2,000 years. This fertile land has witnessed the establishment of the earliest Chinese capitals, the richest ancient remains, and the most magnificent heroic legends.

Henan was also a hub where eastern and western cultures came together and communicated. An ancient trade route started from here, extending across Central Asia to reach India and West Asia, and still farther, to Europe and North Africa. This ancient road was a miracle in the history of human transportation: the human race was never hindered by distances to see and communicate with the world. Countless pioneers travelled over mountains and other barriers to lay roads and create paths for civilizations across the world. In 1877, German geographer Richthofen (fig.1−2) first named this road "the Silk Road". Initially, Richthofen coined the term to refer only to the trade routes between China and West Turkestan and Northwest India

西经中亚，远抵印度、西亚，甚至欧洲和北非。这条古道是人类交通史上的伟大奇迹。遥远的距离并没有阻断人们交流的愿望，无数旅人跨越高山险阻，踏出一条横贯世界东西的文明通道。1877年，德国地理学家李希霍芬（图1-2）用"丝绸之路"来称呼这条古道。最初，李希霍芬创造该词，仅仅指代公元前114年到公元127年之间中国与西土耳其斯坦、西北印度之间的贸易通道。后来这个词语的概念不断扩大，大体上可以视为古代中国与欧亚大陆中西部之间复杂交通网络的总称。

图1-2 "丝绸之路"的提出者李希霍芬
Fig.1-2 Richthofen, the originator of the term "Silk Road"

在漫长的岁月里，这条古道把中国丝绸带给了世界，也把繁荣带给了河南这片热土。

让我们就从这条古道和这片土地说起。

一、繁荣的丝绸之路贸易

让我们把目光投向公元69年的洛阳城。

此时，伟大的历史学家班固，刚刚写就汉大赋最著名的篇章《两都赋》。他用雄壮、华丽的辞藻，比较了长安和洛阳两座城市。长安是西汉王朝的都城，公元8年，西汉政权被外戚王莽篡夺，国家陷入混乱和战争，

between 114 B.C. and 127 A.D. Later on, the definition of "the Silk Road" was expanded to be applicable as a general term for the complex transportation network between ancient China and Midwestern Eurasia.

During many long periods of time, this significant ancient road served as the conduit for Chinese silk going out to the world and brought prosperity to Henan.

Let's start with this ancient road and this land.

I. Prosperity of the Silk Road Trade

Let us look at the City of Luoyang in 69 A.D.

At this point in time, the great historian Ban Gu had just finished his masterpiece, *A Fu about the Two Capitals*, one of the most renowned pieces of fu (an ancient Chinese writing genre of rhymed prose), in which he compared two capital cities, Chang'an and Luoyang, in a splendid and stately rhetoric. Chang'an was the capital of the Western Han Dynasty. In 8 A.D., the throne of the Western Han Dynasty was usurped by Wang Mang, a distant relative of the emperor, and the country fell into chaos and war. Liu Xiu, another relative of the emperor, ended the chaotic situation, re-established the regime and relocated to Luoyang, which is located to the east of Chang'an, and later generations refer to the dynasty of Liu Xiu's regime as "the Eastern Han".

In Ban Gu's writing, the organizational system of the latter capital Luoyang was more coherent with moral standards than the former capital Chang'an, and was thus more commendable. The resurgence of the Han Dynasty, driven by a noble sense of mission, brought together craftsmen and fugitives who evaded the old cities to erect palaces, temples and academies in the wilderness. A new era was launched.

The relocation of the capital during the Eastern Han Dynasty also brought about another effect: Luoyang would take the place of Chang'an as the Silk Road's eastern point of departure.

1. The Early Prosperity of the Henan Silk Road in the Eastern Han Dynasty

After the establishment of the Eastern Han Dynasty, Luoyang became the political, economic and cultural center of the country. During the time of Emperor Ming of the Eastern Han Dynasty, a war against the Huns was won and Ban Chao was appointed the lord in charge of the Western Regions, thus officially restoring the

汉室宗亲刘秀结束了乱局，重建政权并迁都洛阳。因为洛阳位于长安之东，后人遂将刘秀中兴的王朝称作"东汉"。

在班固笔下，新都洛阳的建制要比旧都长安更加符合道德标准，所以更加值得赞许。浴火重生的汉王朝，在一种崇高使命感的驱动下，召集大量工匠和"刑徒"，避开旧有的城市，在旷野上建起宫殿、庙堂和太学，开启一个崭新的时代。

东汉迁都还带来另外一重影响：洛阳将取代长安，成为丝绸之路的东方起点。

1. 东汉时期河南丝绸之路首次繁荣

东汉建立后，洛阳成为全国的政治、经济和文化中心。东汉明帝时期，朝廷击败匈奴，任命班超为西域都护，正式恢复中原与西域各国之间的联系。班超在西域生活31年，赢得西域诸国的尊重和友谊。班超去世后，他的儿子班勇继承了他在西域的事业，继续维持丝绸之路的畅通。班超、班勇父子长期在西域生活，深刻了解丝绸之路沿线各国的情况，《后汉书·西域传》就是根据班勇的记录写成的。

在政治联系加强的基础上，洛阳和西域各国的商业往来也日益频繁。《后汉书·西域传》曾有这样的记载："驰命走驿，不绝于时月；商胡贩客，日款于塞下。"大量的胡商奔走、往来于洛阳，使中原汉地的丝绸等物品源源不断地向洛阳汇集，然后运抵中亚地区及罗马帝国等处。中国的丝绸历经艰险运抵罗马后，被裁成衣服，风靡一时，成为罗马贵族争相穿着炫耀之物。

2. 魏晋南北朝时期河南丝绸之路继续繁荣

魏晋南北朝时期，洛阳长期作为都城，加之统治者十分重视和西域

ties between the Eastern Han Dynasty and the Western Regions, where Ban Chao spent 31 years of his life and won the respect of and friendship with the nations in the Western Regions. After the death of Ban Chao, his son Ban Yong took over his position in the Western Regions and continued to maintain order on the Silk Road. Ban Chao and Ban Yong were stationed in the Western Regions for so many years that they had a deep understanding of the Silk Road adjacent nations. In *The Book of the Later Han*, a volume entitled *The Biography of the Western Regions* was based on historical accounts that were provided by Ban Yong.

Political connections with the Western Regions were strengthened and business contacts increased. As *The Biography of the Western Regions* noted, "Messengers and errand runners ply to and fro, merchants and travelers from the west seek lodgings here every day." A large number of Hu merchants (merchants from the Western Regions) flocked to Luoyang. Large quantities of silk and other commodities sourced from the Central Plains were continuously gathered in Luoyang, and transported to Central Asia, the Roman Empire and other places. Against all kinds of difficulties and dangers, Chinese silk was transported to Rome, and then tailored into dresses and clothes that were extremely popular among the Roman nobility.

2. The Flourishing Prosperity of the Henan Silk Road during the Wei-Jin and Southern-Northern Dynasties

During the Wei-Jin and Southern-Northern Dynasties, Luoyang was the capital of China for a considerably long period of history. The governing lords attached great importance to contacts with the nations in the Western Regions. The Henan Silk Road maintained its former prosperity. During the Western Jin Dynasty, the Central Plains area was politically stable and economically developed. The Western Jin emperor boasted to have "secured diplomatic relations never established before and places never conquered before". When Sima Yan ascended the throne, he held a grand ceremony and thousands of Huns and other Western Regions people came to extend their congratulations.

After the Northern Wei Dynasty moved its capital to Luoyang, on the southern bank of the Luohe River, next to the imperial thoroughfare, there were four lodge mansions, named Jinling, Yanran, Fusang and Yanzi, to accommodate merchants and emissaries from the Western Regions, Japan and other foreign countries. The royal court

各国的联系，河南丝绸之路依旧保持着往日的繁荣景象。西晋时期，中原王朝政治稳定，经济发达，西晋皇帝自夸"通上代之不通，服前王之未服"，司马炎即皇帝位时，在洛阳南郊举行盛大的仪式，前来祝贺的匈奴人及其他西域各国人士有数万人。

北魏迁都洛阳后，在洛河南岸，夹御道有四夷馆，"一名金陵，二名燕然，三名扶桑，四名崦嵫"，安置来自西域以及日本等国的商人和使者。北魏朝廷十分重视丝绸的生产。北魏皇帝曾专门以诏令的形式要求大力发展农桑事业。在北魏统治者的大力推动下，北魏的丝绸业十分发达，国家府库中丝绸堆积盈山，不可较数。这些丝绸除了通过商业贸易传入西域之外，还有一些是通过赠赐的形式传入西域。

3. 隋唐时期河南丝绸之路再次繁荣

隋唐时期，中国结束了长达几百年的分裂、战争局面，社会开始进入一个新的繁荣时期。隋炀帝修建起以洛阳为中心，北达涿郡（今北京），南抵余杭（今杭州）的大运河。借助于隋唐大运河的修建，洛阳成为全国的经济中心。隋炀帝时期，在洛阳的建国门外，设招待四方蛮夷属国酋长、贡使的四方馆。洛阳城中设有通远、丰都、大同三市。三市都傍通河渠，市场店铺装饰得整齐划一，陈列各色珍奇货物。

进入唐代，女皇武则天（图 1-3）统治时期改洛阳为"神都"，并进行营建，洛阳经济繁荣，来到洛阳的使者和商人更多。武则天在洛阳设立专门的国家纺织机构，从花色品种、图案款式等各方面对丝织品进行改进。唐代洛阳的南市占据两坊之地，来自全国各地的商品汇集到南市，再从这里运输到西域各地，成为全国丝绸等重要商品的集散中心。

of the Northern Wei Dynasty attached great importance to the production of silk, and the emperor issued imperial edicts to stress the priority of the silk industry. This was why this industry became a booming economic sector in Northern Wei, where government warehouses were filled with silk to be traded or bestowed to the Western Regions.

3. The Sui and Tang Dynasties, another Prosperous Era of the Silk Road

The Sui and Tang Dynasties witnessed an era of prosperity after hundreds of years of being split, and wars. The Emperor Yang of Sui commanded and supervised the construction of the Grand Canal, which was centered at Luoyang, extending southward to Yuhang (now Hangzhou) and northward to Zhuojun (now Beijing). Luoyang evolved into a commercial center for the country. During this time, a mansion named Sifang was built outside Luoyang's Jianguo Gate, providing accommodation for foreign guests and emissaries. Three well-organized marketplaces, Tongyuan, Fengdu, and Datong, were located along the canal, exhibiting a wide variety of commodities.

In the Tang Dynasty, Empress Wu Zetian (fig. 1–3) renamed Luoyang "Divine Capital" and commanded a massive reconstruction of this city. The economy of Luoyang was booming. More emissaries and businessmen came to visit Luoyang. Wu Zetian established a specialized textile facility to improve the colour, variety and design patterns of silk products. Goods shipped here from all over the country were gathered in a huge marketplace, called the "Southern Market", and transported to the Western Regions and other places. This market served as a national distribution center for silk and other important commodities.

4. New Situation of the Henan Silk Road during the Northern Song Dynasty

During the Northern Song Dynasty, the capital of China was relocated to Kaifeng (regularly referred to as the "Eastern Capital"). The Song Dynasty was a period of mercantilism in ancient China, when both domestic and foreign trade reached their highest levels in the world. The Northern Song Dynasty broke the tradition that urban-based commercial activities were limited to fixed marketplaces and permitted street-side commercial businesses. Business streets duly flourished in Kaifeng City. In the Song Dynasty, some government-sponsored facilities were established in charge of the production of brocades, dyeing, precision manufacturing, embroidery, and so forth. Such facilities were also set up in major silk production places. Meanwhile, private silk production businesses also flourished and lots of rich

图1-3 武则天像
Fig.1-3 A portrait of Wu Zetian

4. 北宋时期河南丝绸之路出现转折

北宋时期,朝廷迁都开封。宋代是中国古代"重商主义"时期,国内外贸易都达到了当时世界上的最高水平。北宋打破了之前城市商业活动必须在固定市场内部进行的传统,允许城市沿街两边经营商业,开封出现了一大批热闹的商业街。宋代朝廷在中央专门设立官营的绫锦院、染院、文思院和文绣院等机构生产丝织品,同时还在重要丝绸产区设置官营织造机构。在官营丝织业发展的同时,城市中的民间丝织作坊也开始大量涌现,出现了很多民间丝绸生产富商。

宋代的丝绸贸易分陆路和海路两部分进行。在陆上贸易方面,北宋主要通过周边的西夏和契丹政权与西域各国进行商业活动。北宋以丝绸、瓷器、茶叶等换取西域各国的马匹等物品。茶叶和马匹等物品的交易量开始在丝绸之路贸易中占据越来越重要的地位。维吾尔族诗人尤甫普在其长诗《福乐智慧》中写道:"大地铺上绿毯,契丹商队运来中国的商品。"这就是描写北宋和西域各国通过契丹人进行商品交易的场景。

北宋丝绸贸易最重要的变化是海上丝绸之路开始兴起,并逐渐繁荣。

merchants emerged.

In the Song Dynasty, silk was shipped by land and by sea. By the land routes, the business was mainly commodity trade with West Xia, Khitan and other Western Regions nations, with which the Northern Song traded silk, china and tea for horses. These commodities were of no less importance than silk on the Silk Road. In his long poem *Happiness and Wisdom*, Uygur poet Yusuf wrote, "The land is covered with green carpet, and goods from China are brought here by Khitan by caravans", referring to the situation of commodity trading between the Northern Song Dynasty and the Western Regions countries via Khitan.

The most important development in the silk trade in the Northern Song Dynasty was the rise and prosperity of the Maritime Silk Road. During the reign of Emperor Taizong of the Song Dynasty, the central government built Fanfang, i.e. facilities for accommodating foreigners, and set up a ministry to supervise foreign trade activities. In the third year of Yuanfeng (1080 A.D.) during the reign of Emperor Shenzong of the Song Dynasty, the Imperial Court issued *Guangzhou Maritime Transport Law*, which was the first special law enacted to regulate non-governmental overseas trade in the world. As the Grand Canal could reach Kaifeng directly from the sea, Kaifeng in the Northern Song Dynasty was not only the administrative center of the Maritime Silk Road, but also the place of departure as well as destination of the Maritime Silk Road. According to a book entitled *Reminiscences of the Eastern Capital*, there were countless stores and shops in Kaifeng City. As many have described, Kaifeng in the Song Dynasty was a "dreamy metropolis".

II. The Prosperous Silk Road Cities

Along the Silk Road, merchants from Europe, West Asia and Central Asia flocked to cities like Luoyang and Kaifeng, bringing about urban prosperity that was rarely seen in other ancient societies.

1. Luoyang, the East Start of the Silk Road, a Place Abundant with Henan Silk Road Relics

Luoyang was historically reputed as "the center of the world" and "the heart of the central land". The Heluo area, centered in Luoyang, is one of Chinese

宋太宗年间，中央政府在重要口岸兴建蕃坊让外国商人居住，并设蕃长管理对外商务活动。宋神宗元丰三年（公元1080年），朝廷颁布《广州市舶条法》，这是世界上首部为民间海外贸易设立的专门法规。由于大运河能够直接从海上到达开封，所以北宋时期的开封既是海上丝绸之路的管理地，更是海上丝绸之路的出发地、目的地。据《东京梦华录》描述，开封城里店铺鳞次栉比，商品琳琅满目。北宋的开封，恍如仙境，被称为"梦一样的城市"。

二、繁华的丝绸之路城市

循着丝绸之路，来自欧洲、西亚和中亚的商旅云集在洛阳、开封等城市，带来古代社会难得一见的城市繁荣景象。

1. 洛阳——丝绸之路东起点，河南丝路文化遗迹集中地

洛阳素有"天下之中""九州腹地"之称，以洛阳为中心的河洛地区是华夏文明的重要发祥地。洛河两岸，在不足30公里的范围内，分布着二里头遗址、偃师商城遗址、东周王城遗址、汉魏洛阳故城和隋唐洛阳城遗址五大都城遗址，人称"五都贯洛"。都城遗址如此密集，联系如此密切，时间跨度又如此之大，这在全世界绝无仅有。目前，除东周王城遗址外，其余四遗址均被国家列为大遗址保护项目。2010年，中国国家文物局公布了第一批国家考古遗址公园名单，隋唐洛阳城遗址成功入选，汉魏洛阳故城被列入立项名单。2017年，中国国家文物局公布了第三批国家考古遗址公园名单，偃师商城遗址、二里头遗址被列入立项名单。

汉魏洛阳故城位于今洛阳市区以东约15公里处，位于洛阳市洛龙区、孟津县、偃师市交界处，始建于西周初年，废弃于唐初，前后延续使用长达1500多年。东周、东汉、曹魏、西晋、北魏等朝代先后以此作为国都，

civilization's places of origin. On both sides of the Luohe River, within less than 30 kilometers, there are archeological sites, including the Erlitou Ruins, the Yanshi Shang City Ruins, the Zhou Imperial City, the Han-Wei Ancient City, and the Sui-Tang Luoyang City Ruins. Together they are known as "a conglomerate of five capitals in Heluo area". So concentrated and closely related are these ancient capital cities located in Luoyang, and enjoy a profoundly long span of history. This is incomparable in the world. Presently, except for the relics of Zhou Imperial City, the other four sites have been listed as major historic relics protection projects by the state. In 2010, China's National Cultural Heritage Administration announced the first list of national archaeological sites, which included the Sui-Tang Luoyang City Ruins and the Han-Wei Ancient City. In 2017, the National Cultural Heritage Administration issued the list of the third batch of national archaeological site parks, which included the Yanshi Shang City Ruins, and the Erlitou Ruins.

Located 15 kilometers to the east of present Luoyang City and at what is now the intersection of Luolong District, Mengjin County and Yanshi City, the Han-Wei Ancient City of Luoyang was built in the early Western Zhou Dynasty and abandoned in the early Tang Dynasty. For over 1,500 years, it functioned as the national capital of the Eastern Zhou Dynasty, the Eastern Han Dynasty, the Cao Wei Dynasty, the Western Jin Dynasty, the Northern Wei Dynasty, and other dynasties. The history of Luoyang being the national capital exceeds 540 years, the longest among Chinese cities that functioned as national capitals. At the best of its times, the Han-Wei Ancient City of Luoyang was 10 kilometers in both length and width, covering an area of approximately 100 square kilometers. It was the largest ancient capital city in the world.

Located about 10 kilometers west of the Han-Wei Ancient City of Luoyang, the Sui-Tang Luoyang City (fig.1－4) is a large-scale ancient city site preserved from the Sui and Tang Dynasties. It was built in the initial year of the Sui Dynasty (605 A.D.) and was then serving as the capital, or secondary capital, during the Tang Dynasty, the Five Dynasties and the Northern Song Dynasty periods. It was named Luoyang Palace, Eastern Capital and Devine Capital consecutively, and it functioned as the national capital for as long as over 500 years. The site of Luoyang City in the Sui and Tang Dynasties covered an area of about 47 square kilometers across the banks of the Luohe River. It was mainly composed of eight parts: the Palace City,

都城史长达540多年,是我国历史上定都总时间最长的古城遗址。鼎盛时,汉魏洛阳城长、宽各10公里,面积约100平方公里,是世界上面积最大的古代都城。

隋唐洛阳城遗址(图1-4)位于汉魏洛阳城以西约10公里处,是我国现存隋唐时期保存较为完整的大型古代城市遗址。隋唐洛阳城始建于隋大业元年(公元605年),唐、五代和北宋时期仍为都城或陪都,先后被称为洛阳宫、东都、神都、东京,其沿用时间长达五百余年。隋唐洛阳城遗址地跨洛河南北两岸,面积约47平方公里,主要由宫城、皇城、外郭城、东城、含嘉仓城、上阳宫、西苑、离宫八部分组成。遗址以洛河为界,分南北两个区域:洛河以北主要是宫城核心区,占地约1 300亩,主要保护展示明堂、天堂、应天门和九洲池等重要遗址;洛河以南为里坊区,占地约7平方公里。明堂位于隋唐洛阳城宫城核心区内,是武则天的宫城正殿,建于公元687年,初名"万象神宫",重建后曰"通天宫",是武则天举行重大礼仪活动、颁布政令、举行祭祀活动的重要场所。明堂是历史上体量最大之木构建筑,高约90米,是唐代建筑的巅峰之作。天堂始

图1-4 隋唐洛阳城遗址 摄影:李伟年

Fig.1-4 The reconstruction based on the relics of the Sui-Tang Luoyang City

the Imperial City, the Exterior City, the Eastern City, the City of Hanjia Granary, the Shangyang Palace, the west garden and an imperial dwelling palace outside of the city. The Sui-Tang Luoyang City is divided by the Luohe River into two parts. The core area of the Palace City is to the north of the river. Covering 1,300 acres, it primarily comprises the Ming Palace, the Heaven Palace, Yingtian Gate and Jiuzhou Pond. To the south are the ancient neighborhood blocks, covering approximately 7 square kilometers. The Ming Palace, built in 687 A.D., was located in the central area of the Palace City, serving as Empress Wu Zetian's main palace, which was initially named "Cosmos Palace" and was renamed "Heavenly Supreme Palace" after a reconstruction. This palace was where Wu Zetian's ceremonies were celebrated, imperial edicts were issued, and spring-autumn sacrificial rites were held. The Ming Palace was the largest wood building in history, about 90 meters high, a masterpiece of Tang Dynasty architecture. The Heavenly Palace, located next to and north of the Ming Palace, began to be constructed in 689 A.D. This Palace was devoted to Wu Zetian's Buddhist worship activities.

Dingding (Cauldron Setting, signifying the establishment of a capital) Gate was the southern and main gate of the Exterior City of Luoyang during the Sui and Tang Dynasties. It was a landmark on the central axis of the Sui-Tang Luoyang City. The gate was officially built and opened in the second year of the Sui Dynasty (606 A.D.). After that, it was designated as the southern gate of the Exterior City in the Tang Dynasty, the Later Liang, the Later Tang, the Later Zhou and the Northern Song Dynasties. Serving as the capital's main gate for 530 years, this gate enjoys the longest history among ancient Chinese capital city gates.

2. Kaifeng, a Junction of Water and Road Transportation, a Dream Place on the Silk Road

Kaifeng, historically known as Daliang, Bianzhou, the Eastern Capital, Bian Capital, Bianliang, etc., is commonly abbreviated as Bian. Kaifeng enjoys a history of more than 4,100 years. Designated state capital eight times (the Xia Dynasty, the State of Wei in the Warring States Era, the Later Liang, the Later Jin, the Later Han, the Later Zhou, the Northern Song and the Jin Dynasties), Kaifeng is known as the eight-dynasty capital. During the Yuan, Ming and Qing Dynasties, and the early period of the Republic of China, until the initial period after the foundation of People's Republic of China, Kaifeng functioned as the provincial capital of Henan

建于公元 689 年，位于明堂北侧，是武则天的御用礼佛圣地。

定鼎门是隋唐洛阳城外郭城的正南门，是隋唐洛阳城中轴线上的标志性建筑。城门正式启用于隋大业二年（公元 606 年），之后，相继被唐、后梁、后唐、后周和北宋定为外郭城正南门，沿用时间长达 530 年，是迄今为止发现的沿用时间最长的中国古代都城城门。

2. 开封——水陆交汇之都，丝绸之路梦华之地

开封，古称大梁、汴州、东京、汴京、汴梁等，简称汴。开封迄今已有 4 100 余年的建城史，夏朝，战国时的魏，五代时期的后梁、后晋、后汉、后周，北宋和金朝相继在此定都，被誉为"八朝古都"。从元明清到民国再到中华人民共和国成立初期，开封一直为河南首府或省会，是世界上唯一一座城市中轴线从未变动的都城。

因黄河泥沙淤积使黄河河床不断抬高，开封出现了河高于城的"地上悬河"。历次黄河水患使开封数座古都城、府州城池深深埋于地面之下 3 米至 12 米处，上下叠压着 6 座城池，其中包括 3 座都城、2 座省城、1 座州城，构成了中国罕见的"城摞城"奇特景观，这在世界考古史和都城史上都是少有的。开封是享誉中国的著名民间艺术之乡，享有"中国戏曲之乡""中国木版年画之乡""中国菊花之乡"等美誉，有官瓷、朱仙镇木版年画等精美工艺品。

北宋开封城分外城、里城和皇城三重。外城南墙南门与里城的南门、宫城南门纵贯成直线，构成全城的中轴线，称御街。御街宽约 280 米，中心有砖石砌成的御沟水两道，种植莲荷桃李等植物，春夏之间，望之如绣。里城是今开封城的前身。宋徽宗时，在里城东北隅修筑人工山，名万岁山，用太湖石堆积而成，四方花竹奇石皆集于此，穷极巧妙。皇城正殿为大庆殿，位于宣德门之里，位于全城的中轴线上，殿庭广阔，宏伟壮丽，可以容纳数万人。

北宋开封城是四条河流——金水河、五丈河、汴河、蔡河通过的地方，

Province, and is the only capital city where the geographic axis has never been altered.

Because of the geographic conditions of sand and mud in the Yellow River, the riverbed of the Yellow River has been elevated continuously, and Kaifeng has developed "suspended river above the land level" terrain conditions. Underground in Kaifeng, several ancient capitals were buried 3 to 12 meters deep because of the Yellow River floods. Six cities, including three capitals, two provincial cities and one prefecture, stacked one on top of the other, constituting a peculiar stack of ancient city relics, which is very rare in China and in the history of archaeology. Kaifeng is a well-known folk-art town in China, enjoying the reputation of the "hometown of Chinese folk opera", the "hometown of Chinese woodcut new-year pictures", the "hometown of the Chinese chrysanthemum", and the hometown of other fine handicrafts such as porcelain produced by official kilns, and the Zhuxian Township wood cut new-year pictures.

Kaifeng City in the Northern Song Dynasty was divided into three parts: the Outer City, the Inner City and the Palace City. The gate of the southern wall of the Outer City was aligned with the southern gate of the Inner City and the southern gate of the Palace City, and this alignment constituted the central axis of the whole city, known as the Royal Street. The Royal Street was about 280 meters wide. Two water channels ran along the Royal Street, where lotus, peaches and plums were planted, as beautiful as a piece of embroidery in spring and summer. The Inner City was the predecessor of Kaifeng today. During the reign of the Emperor Hui of the Song Dynasty, an artificial hill named Longevity Hill was built in the northeastern corner of the Inner City. The hill was built with Taihu Lake rocks (a kind of decorative rock). A treasure of fancy rare rocks and plants gathered together in an ingeniously designed landscape. The main hall of the Palace City was Daqing Palace, located inside the Xuande Gate and on the central axis of the city. The square outside the palace was spacious, with the capacity for tens of thousands of people.

Kaifeng in the Northern Song Dynasty was located where four waterways traversed, including the Jinshui River, the Wuzhang River, the Bian River and the Cai River. Shipping business thrived and commodities trading boomed. Business activities were not restricted to certain regions and there were several night markets where businesses were open all night. Zhang Zeduan, a famous painter during the Northern Song Dynasty, preserved with a piece of painting the city's features and the

河运发达，商业繁荣。百姓、商人经商不受空间约束和时间限制，形成了专业性的夜市。这些夜市通宵营业，买卖昼夜不绝。北宋著名画家张择端的《清明上河图》（图1-5）以长卷形式，生动记录了北宋汴京的城市面貌和当时社会各阶层人民的生活状况。画中各行各业，士农工商，无所不有。大街小巷店铺林立，百肆杂陈，真实再现了北宋开封城的繁华景象。美国耶鲁大学教授乔纳森·斯彭斯曾在《新闻周刊》上刊登文章，他写道："上一个中国世纪是11世纪。当时，中国是世界上最大也是最成功的国家……当时宋朝的首都在东京汴梁，即现在的河南开封，人口达百万，是世界最先进、最繁荣、最庞大的城市。"

图1-5 清明上河图
Fig.1-5 Riverside Scene at the Qingming Festival

作为著名的丝绸之路城市，开封至今还有制作"汴绣"的传统。"汴绣"来自于北宋的"宫廷绣"，以在丝绸上刺绣山水、花鸟、虫鱼等图案为主要特色，有"国宝"之称。宋朝之后，"汴绣"在继承宋代刺绣题材、工艺的基础上，借鉴了其他绣艺的长处，形成了绣工精致细腻、色彩古朴典雅、形象逼真的特色。1959年，汴绣《清明上河图》被作为国庆十周年献礼陈列在人民大会堂，先后获得多个荣誉称号。

living conditions of all kinds of people up and down the social scale. His long volume painting, *Riverside Scene at the Qingming Festival* (fig. 1—5), depicts streets and alleys lined with shops, showing people and tradesmen of all kinds, officials, peasants, workers, business people and so forth. It is a vivid reproduction of the prosperity of Kaifeng during the Northern Song Dynasty. As Yale Professor Jonathan Spence described in an issue of *Newsweek*, "the last China's century was the 11th century, when China was the largest and the most successful nation in the world… Kaifeng, then known as Bianliang, was the most advanced, the most prosperous and the largest city in the world."

As a famous Silk Road City, Kaifeng still has the tradition of making "Bian Embroidery", which originated from the "Royal Embroidery" of the Northern Song Dynasty. This embroidery style, renowned as a "national treasure", is characterized by the embroidery of silk depicting the images of landscapes, flowers, birds, insects, fish, etc. After the Song Dynasty, Bian embroidery not only inherited previously popular subject matters and techniques,but also assimilated the strengths of other embroidery styles and evolved into an exquisite embroidery genre, characterized by its simplicity, its elegant colors and layering, as well as its imagery and vividness. In 1959, an embroidery piece reproducing *Riverside Scene at the Qingming Festival* was created to celebrate the 10th anniversary of the People's Republic of China, and it was exhibited in the Great Hall of the People. This amazing piece of embroidery won various top-grade Chinese art awards.

3. Zhengzhou, a Birthplace of Chinese Silk, and an Important Station on the New Silk Road

Zhengzhou, one of Chinese civilization's places of origin was the chief territory of "three Sovereigns and five Emperors" in the prehistoric times. Over 3,600 years ago, Zhengzhou served as the capital of the Shang Dynasty in its early period and was where Yin-Shang culture originated. Zhengzhou's ancient Shang City was the ruins of a capital city of the Shang Dynasty, which began to be built about 1,500 B.C. Located presently in Guancheng district of Zhengzhou, the Shang City ruins covers a rectangular territory. Compared with other ancient capital relics of the Shang and Zhou Dynasties, the Shang City is a big one. In 1046 B.C., after the Zhou Dynasty conquered the Shang Dynasty, Guanshu was designated the lord in charge of this territory, which was thus named the State of Guan.

3.郑州——中国丝绸发明地，"新丝绸之路"上的重要驿站

郑州是中华文明的发祥地之一，是三皇五帝活动的主要区域，早在3 600余年前就成为中国商代早中期都城，是殷商文明的重要发源地。郑州古商城是商代早中期的都城，该城始建于公元前1500年前后，商城遗址位于今郑州市管城区内，商城平面近似长方形，与已发掘的商周时期的其他城池相比，其规模称得上是较大的。公元前1046年，周灭殷商建立西周，封管叔于郑州，称管国。

郑州为轩辕黄帝故里。据历史传说和史书记载，黄帝的正妃嫘祖（出生地为今河南省西平县）曾经在这里发明并传播植桑养蚕、缫丝等技术，被后人尊为"蚕神""衣神"。1983年在郑州荥阳市青台遗址考古发掘中发现的炭化丝织物，为嫘祖"育蚕、取丝、造机杼作衣"的传说提供了实物佐证。郑州是中国丝绸发明地之一，是最早的丝绸生产和传播中心，是古老丝绸之路的重要节点，在历史上是丝绸、茶叶、陶瓷通过丝绸之路外运前的必经之地和暂留地。郑州市站街镇大、小黄冶村附近黄河两岸的唐三彩窑址是已知最早、规模最大的唐三彩窑场。

作为中国最重要的陆路交通枢纽之一，郑州在"新丝绸之路"沿线城市的经济文化发展中具有十分重要的作用，已成为"新丝绸之路"中国公路快速通道上的重要驿站。全长4 395公里的连霍国道主干线是中国最长的高速公路，沿"古丝绸之路"不断向西延伸，经中亚和欧洲诸国直到大西洋，构成了对亚欧大陆经贸活动发挥巨大作用的"新丝绸之路"。

4.三门峡——丝绸之路的交通咽喉，古道、古关独具特色

三门峡地区的义马、渑池、灵宝一线，是中原通往西域的交通咽喉，

Zhengzhou was the home place of the Yellow Emperor. According to relevant historical literature and legends, the Yellow Emperor's wife Madam Lei once invented and disseminated silk weaving techniques in Zhengzhou, such as mulberry cultivation, silkworm breeding, silk extraction, etc. Therefore, she was worshipped as the goddess in charge of silkworm farming and clothing. Carbonized silk fabrics discovered in the archaeological excavation of the Qingtai relic site in Xingyang (a borough of Zhengzhou) in 1983 provided solid evidence for the legend of Madam Lei's "rearing silkworms, extracting silk and making clothes using specialized machines". Zhengzhou is one of the places where Chinese silk was invented, the earliest center of silk production and distribution, and the ultimate origin of the ancient Silk Road. Zhengzhou was historically a Silk Road distribution center where commodities such as silk, tea and porcelain were temporarily stored. The Tang Sancai (tri-colored glazed porcelain of the Tang Dynasty) kiln remains on both banks of the Yellow River near Dahuangye Village and Xiaohuangye Village in Zhanjie Township of Zhengzhou are the relics of the earliest and largest known Tang Sancai kilns.

As one of the most important land transportation hubs in China, Zhengzhou plays an important role in the economic and cultural development of the cities along the "New Silk Road", and is one of the most important stations of the "New Silk Road" China Expressway. The 4,395-kilometer-long Lianhuo Highway (the expressway linking Lianyungang City in Jiangsu Province and Horgos, a land port in Xinjiang Uygur Autonomous Region), extending westward along the ancient Silk Road, passes through Central Asia and European countries all the way to the Atlantic Ocean. This road, a bona fide new Silk Road, plays a very important part in the economic and trade activities across the Asian and European continents.

4. Sanmenxia, a Silk Road Traffic Hub Characterized by its Unique Ancient Roads and Passes

The area covering Yima, Mianchi and Lingbao in Sanmenxia used to be the key corridor on the way from the Central Plains to the Western Regions during ancient times, and the only passage of East-West traffic. The military powers who tried to seize supremacy over Guanzhong (presently the middle area of Shaanxi Province) or the Central Plains all fought for the control of the Xiaohan Route in Sanmenxia because of its strategic position. On this route, the Xiaohan fortress located to the east of Chang'an and the west of Luoyang served as a security barrier

是东西交通的必经之道。历史上无论何人称雄关中或入主中原，三门峡地区的崤函古道，都因其险要而成为兵家必争之地。崤函古塞，是西京长安以东，东都洛阳以西的屏障和门户，更是古丝绸之路商品和文化传出与输入的必经之地。历经千年岁月的磨砺，在这条古老的通道上，留下了许多与丝绸之路有关的古道、古关等历史文化遗产。

三门峡崤函古道前后延续数千年之久，在保证丝绸之路畅通和促进东西方的交流方面具有重要的地位。现存的石壕古道遗迹（图1-6）是崤函古道东段的一部分，路面为石灰岩质，因车轮长期碾轧，路面上形成了两条较深的车辙印迹，石壕古道因此而得名。古道位于今三门峡市陕州区硖石乡车壕村东南1公里处的山坡上，西北东南走向，全长230米，车辙印迹宽窄不等，深浅不一，最宽处达8.8米，最窄处5.2米，最深处达0.41米，最浅处仅有数厘米。道上留下的车辙印迹有一车道、二车道、三车道。崤函古道虽历经沧桑，但得到了较好的保存，是中国丝绸之路的一处实物标本，也是丝绸之路上真实、完整、原始、海内外少有的一处"路"的遗迹。因此，在《世界遗产名录》里，崤函古道被定性为"丝绸之路上唯一的道路遗产"。

图1-6 石壕古道

Fig.1-6 The Stone Ruts Ancient Road

and transportation portal, which was the only pathway of commercial and cultural activities. There remain many relics of the Silk Road related roads and passes on this ancient route.

The Sanmenxia Xiaohan Route witnessed thousands of years of history and played an important role in guaranteeing the traffic flow and continuity of trade activities between the east and the west. Part of the Xiaohan Route, a limestone road, is marked with two deep wheel ruts, hence the name "the Stone Ruts Ancient Road" (fig. 1−6). Located near a village named Vehicle Ruts Village in Shanzhou District of Sanmenxia, this road goes in a southeast direction, 230 meters in length, 5.2 meters at its narrowest point, and 8.8 meters at its widest point. The depth of the ruts ranges from several centimeters to 0.41 meters. The ruts make visible the traces of single lanes, double lanes and triple lanes. Despite vicissitudes and tribulations, the authenticity and integrity of the ancient Xiaohan Route have been well preserved. It is a genuine specimen of the Silk Road and also a real, complete, primitive and rare road relic of the Silk Road. Therefore, in the *World Heritage List*, the Xiaohan Ancient Route is recognized as the only road heritage of the Silk Road.

5. Nanyang, a Terminal of "Ships from the South and Horses from the North" Abundant with Cultural Heritages of the Silk Road

Nanyang historically functioned as a significant terminal of transit to and from all directions. There are profuse cultural remains of the Silk Road in this area. Nanyang's Fangcheng County is located in the northeastern area of the Nanyang Basin. The Fangcheng Pass provided the only natural passage for transportation by road and commercial activities on the way from the Nanyang Basin to the Central Plains. The Great Wall of Chu in Fangcheng was the first ancient long wall in the world. The Zeng Pass was the only passage between the Central Plains and the region covering Jingzhou and Xiangyang. In the Xia-Shang relics site found in Fangcheng, stone axes, weaving wheels and steam cookers were unearthed. A large number of Han Dynasty stone figures of the Hu people (fig. 1−7) were excavated in Fangcheng and its surrounding areas.

Ⅲ. Advanced Silk Road Transportation

As Luoyang served as the national capital of ancient China for long periods of

5.南阳——南船北马中转站，丝路文化遗存丰厚

南阳自古为南北东西交通的"大转盘"、南船北马的中转站，保存有相当丰富的丝绸之路文化遗迹。南阳市的方城县地处南阳盆地东北缘，方城垭口是南阳盆地北通中原唯一的天然陆路通道，是古商路上的天然关隘。方城楚长城为天下第一古长城，方城的缯关为北出中原、南通荆襄的门户和唯一通道。方城境内发现的夏商遗址中出土有石钺、纺轮、蒸汽甑等重要文物。方城及周边地区曾出土大量的胡人形象的汉代画像石（图1-7）。

图1-7 南阳汉画

Fig.1-7 A stone inscribed art piece of Han Dynasty style unearthed in Nanyang

三、发达的丝绸之路交通

由于洛阳长期是古代中国的都城，所以河南境内的丝绸之路主要围绕洛阳展开。以洛阳为中心的丝绸之路主要由京洛道、汴洛道、大运河、

time, the Silk Road routes in Henan were chiefly centered at Luoyang. This part of the Silk Road comprised the Jingluo Route (Chang'an to Luoyang), the Bianluo Route (Bianjing to Luoyang), the Great Canal, the Wanluo Route (Nanyang to Luoyang) and the Taihang Tunnel Roads.

1. The Jingluo Route

The Jingluo Route refers to the Chang'an to Luoyang section of the Silk Road, and also the main trunk of the Silk Road in Henan. The Jingluo Route, starting from Luoyang, was composed of two branches: the northern line and the southern line. The northern line went westward from the Hangu Pass of Han and the southern line went westward along the Luohe River, then the two lines converged on the southern bank of the Yellow River, continued into Shaanxi through the Tong Pass, and then went down the narrow corridor between the Qinling Mountains and the Wei River, and finally reached Chang'an. Before the Anshi Rebellion (a prolonged unrest triggered by the rebellion instigated by An Lushan and carried on by Shi Siming in the Tang Dynasty), the emperors and officials of the Sui and Tang Dynasties often went on trips between Luoyang and Chang'an. The road conditions were fairly decent. In order for the emperor to stay and rest en route, a number of palaces were built. These palaces, of which the names were well-documented, include Huaqing, Xiuling, Zigui, Lanfeng, and so on. The road was lined with trees on both sides, in order to beautify the views and scenery. As a Baijuyi's poem goes, "The state road (state-administered road) is well-shaded by willows, and palaces decorated by profuse flowers."

According to the Tang Dynasty standard, a courier station was set up at every 30-li (Chinese mile) interval along the state roads. These courier stations were managed by state-appointed functionaries, whose duties were to provide accommodation and assistance for travelling officials. With there being over 350 kilometers between Luoyang and Chang'an, there were 40-odd courier stations along the Jingluo Route. Among them, the Linquanyi Station near the Luohe River was a subject matter recurrently appearing in Tang Dynasty poems. During the Anshi Rebellion, after Shi Siming's defeat, he and his troops fled along this road and were captured at a courier station named "Luqiaoyi", then were executed at the Linquanyi Station. They both were located in what is now Luoning County.

Due to its ancient history, there are not many visible remains of the Silk Road in

宛洛道、太行孔道等道路组成。

1. 京洛道

京洛道是河南丝绸之路的主干，是丝绸之路洛阳至长安段的另一种称谓。京洛道从洛阳出发，以崤山为界，分为南北两线。北线出汉函谷关西行，南线沿洛水而西，然后两条路线在黄河南岸汇合，经潼关进入陕西，再穿过秦岭、渭水南的狭长走廊，通向长安。安史之乱以前，隋唐两代帝王和官员常在洛阳、长安之间往来，道路条件很好。为便于帝王在沿途停留休息，一路上建有多处行宫，名称可考的有华清、绣岭、紫桂、兰峰、崎岫、福昌、连昌、显仁、甘泉、连曜等等。为美化沿途环境，官府在道旁种植槐、柳等树木。白居易的诗句"官道柳荫荫，行宫花漠漠"，便是描写京洛道旁槐柳成荫的景色。

依照唐制，官道每三十里设置一座驿站，由国家任命的驿长管理，负责供给官员往来的食宿。洛阳到长安大约350公里的路途间，设有四十余处驿站。其中洛河附近的临泉驿，唐代诗人题咏甚多。安史之乱中，史思明兵败后沿这条道路逃窜，在鹿桥驿被捉，在临泉驿被杀。两处驿站都在今洛宁县境内。

由于年代久远，隋唐以前河南境内丝绸之路的地面遗存已经不多。洛阳市宜阳县有一座孤独矗立的五花寺塔，坐落在唐代行宫连昌宫的旧址上。一般认为，这座塔是宋人在唐代旧址上重新修葺的。也许当年的行人走在京洛道上，曾经瞻仰着高耸的宝塔，艳羡过行宫的富丽与奢华。现存京洛道最显眼的地标，是位于洛阳市新安县的汉函谷关。此关虽然历经两千多年的风雨剥蚀，关城遗址依然屹立。关前的古道一面临水、一面依山，宽度仅容一车通行，两条车辙深深地印入坚硬的石路。这条通道沿崤山北麓延伸，至今沿用不废。隋唐古路南侧是一条平整的柏油省道，北侧则是繁忙的陇海线，三条交通线平行地排列着。关前"鸡鸣台""望气台"

Henan dating from the time prior to the Sui and Tang Dynasties. There is however a solitary pagoda belonging to Wuhua Temple in Yiyang County of Luoyang, which is situated on the site of the Tang Dynasty's Lianchang Palace. It is generally believed that the tower was originally built in the Tang Dynasty and restored in the Song Dynasty. Pedestrians on the Jingluo Route were certainly impressed by the splendor and magnificence of this pagoda. The most prominent landmark of the Jingluo Route was the Hangu Pass, located in Xin'an County of Luoyang. Despite being eroded by wind and rain for two thousand years, its ruins are still standing. The ancient road alongside the Hangu Pass was next to a river on one side, and a hill on the other. Its width is that of only one vehicle. Two ruts are still visible on the hard-stone road surface. This road extends along the northern foot of Mount Xiao and is still in use. Close to the south side of this ancient road, now there is a well paved road, and to the north is the busy Longhai railway. Three traffic lines are spaced in parallel. The ruins of Jiming Tower and Wangqi Tower, two Han Dynasty watchtowers, still stand before the pass, reflecting and depicting the ancient Han buildings' historical images.

Hangu Pass was not only one of the most famous passes in Chinese history, but also a sacred place for Taoism in China. It was composed of three passes, in three different dynasties, Qin, Han and Wei. The Hangu Pass of Qin (fig.1–8), located in Lingbao City of Henan Province, closely guarded the roads winding through the Xiaohan mountainous areas. The newest Wei Gate is now submerged in the Sanmenxia Reservoir. According to Taoist legend, Lao Tzu, the founder of Taoism in the pre-Qin Dynasty, quit his bureaucratic position and rode an alleged "green buffalo" out of Hangu Pass, heading westward. At that time, Yinxi, a sentinel stationed at Hangu Pass, saw purple clouds coming from the eastern sky and knew that a saint would pass through the gate. He begged Lao Tzu for his teachings, and Lao Tzu taught him the *Tao Te Ching*. Yinxi passed on Lao Tzu's teachings and became the founder of the Taoist Lou Guan School. The Wangqi (meaning "spotting the purple clouds") Tower in front of Hangu Pass was a building that was built in memory of this legend. The Jiming (meaning "rooster's crow") Tower, opposite the Wangqi Tower, was named after a Warring States aristocrat, Meng Changjun. The legend claims that one of his retainers deceived the sentinels of Hangu Pass by imitating a rooster crow and fled the pass in the middle of the night. *The Anthology of Tang Dynasty Writings* collected an *Exit Clearance Issued to an Emissary*

两座汉阙还留有半截残迹，日落时分看去，颇有"西风残照，汉家陵阙"的意境。

函谷关不仅是中国历史上最著名的关塞之一，也是中国本土宗教道教的圣地。它分为秦关、汉关和魏关三座不同时期的关城：秦关（图1-8）位于河南省灵宝市，和汉关一样扼守着崤山间的孔道。时代最晚的魏关现在已经淹没在三门峡水库中。道教传说中，道家学说的创始人老子辞官以后独自骑着一头青牛出函谷关西行。当时把守函谷关的关令尹喜望见东方天上有紫气飘来，知道有圣人过关，于是恳请老子留下教诲，于是老子将自己的学说《道德经》传授给他。尹喜让《道德经》流传天下，他自己也成为道教楼观派的祖师。汉函谷关前的"望气台"就是为纪念这个传说而修建的建筑。"望气台"对面的"鸡鸣台"，则得名于战国时的贵族孟尝君派门客冒充鸡鸣，骗过守关士兵半夜出逃的典故。《全唐文》收录过一篇《恩赐绫锦出关判》，内容是唐代一份关于西域商旅通过函谷关的法律文书。来自安息的使者莫贺，携带美玉来洛阳朝觐，皇帝赐给他大量贵重丝织品让他携带回国。这是"贡赐贸易"的一个生动例证。

图1-8 三门峡灵宝秦函谷关

Fig.1-8 The Hangu Pass of Qin (located in Lingbao of Sanmenxia)

Carrying Emperor-Granted Silk, which provided a Parthian emissary named Mo He a clearance to leave the country. Mo He had brought some fine jade as a tribute to the emperor, and the emperor granted Mo He some fine silk for him to take home. This is a typical case of "tribute trade".

The Jingluo Route was also the only way for merchants and travelers to journey between the two capitals. The prosperity of the avenues in and around Luoyang during the Tang Dynasty is depicted in the *Food and Money* volume of *Tongdian* (an encyclopedic history of institutions) as follows: "Numerous shops and eateries line the streets, catering and entertaining the travelers. They mostly provide donkey rental services for long distance travelers." According to this depiction, the Jingluo Route was at that time a well-conditioned, prosperous and busy thoroughfare.

2. The Sui-Tang Grand Canal

The Sui-Tang Grand Canal was a water transport network centered at Luoyang. The canal stretched from its northern end in Zhuo County (now Beijing), to its southern end in Yuhang (now Hangzhou). This canal was the main conduit between the Land Silk Road and the Maritime Silk Road. It was under the command of the Emperor Yang of the Sui Dynasty that the canal was constructed between 605 A.D. to 610 A.D. It took more than a million laborers and six years to accomplish the whole project. The Sui-Tang Grand Canal was a 2,700-kilometer-long north-south canal which connected the Haihe River, the Yellow River, the Huaihe River, the Yangtze River and the Qiantang River via the Tongji Canal, the Yongji Canal, the Shanyangdu Canal and the Jiangnan Canal. Luoyang, Zhuo County (now Beijing), Bianzhou (now Kaifeng), Songzhou (now Shangqiu), Yuhang (now Hangzhou), Kuaiji (now Shaoxing) and other regional centers were linked together, thus strengthening the connections and transportation between various regions of the country. Luoyang was the only intersection between the Land Silk Road and the Sui-Tang Grand Canal.

The Sui-Tang Grand Canal spanned over 10 degrees of latitude, stretching from the most fertile Northern Chinese Plains to the southeastern coast of China. The canal spanned across Beijing, Tianjin, Hebei, Shandong, Henan, Anhui, Jiangsu and Zhejiang. It was the artery of transportation between the north and the south in ancient China, and the earliest and largest canal in the world. On June 22, 2014, three water ways and ten canal sections, including the Sui-Tang Grand Canal, the

京洛道也是普通商旅、行人往来两京之间的必由之路。《通典·食货》记载过唐代洛阳四周大道的繁荣，"夹路列店肆待客，酒馔丰溢，每店皆有驴赁客乘，倏忽数十里，谓之驿驴"。可见当年这是一条行人络绎、车马喧阗的大路，条件相当完备。

2. 隋唐大运河

隋唐大运河是一条以洛阳为中心，北达涿郡（今北京），南至余杭（今杭州）的水运网络，是连接陆上丝绸之路和海上丝绸之路的主要纽带。隋炀帝于公元605年至公元610年征调百余万人，费时六年才使其全线贯通。隋唐大运河是总长2 700公里的中国南北大运河，它通过通济渠、永济渠、山阳渎和江南运河四大渠道，沟通了海河、黄河、淮河、长江、钱塘江五大水系，并把洛阳、涿郡（今北京）、汴州（今开封）、宋州（今商丘）、余杭（今杭州）、会稽（今绍兴）等区域中心联系在一起，从而加强了各地区间的联系。洛阳是陆上丝绸之路与隋唐大运河唯一的交汇点。

隋唐大运河跨越地球10多个纬度，纵贯中国最富饶的华北平原和东南沿海，地跨北京、天津、河北、山东、河南、安徽、江苏、浙江8个省、直辖市，是中国古代南北交通的大动脉，是世界上开凿最早、规模最大的运河。2014年6月22日，包括隋唐大运河、京杭大运河、浙东运河在内的三大部分十段河道被列入世界文化遗产，成为中国第46个世界遗产项目。隋唐大运河的遗址大体分两种：一种是在地面上，如沿岸的古城镇；另一种是在地下，包括考古挖掘出来的古桥、古码头、古仓窖和古瓷器。

天津桥是隋唐大运河洛阳段的重要附属遗存，位于隋唐洛阳城皇城以南、应天门至定鼎门的连线上，是隋唐洛阳城中轴线的重要组成部分和城市格局的重要地标，前后延续600余年，遗址位于今洛阳桥西约400米的河床内。天津桥初建于隋大业三年（公元607年），原是一座浮桥，隋

Beijing-Hangzhou Grand Canal, and the Eastern Zhejiang Canal, were listed as a World Cultural Heritage, as the 46th World Heritage Project of China. The relics of the Sui-Tang Grand Canal fall into two categories: some are still there above ground, such as the ancient towns along the canal bank, while some are to be, or have been excavated, such as ancient bridges, wharfs, warehouses and porcelain unearthed by archaeologists.

Tianjin Bridge is an important subsidiary relic of the Luoyang section of the Sui-Tang Grand Canal. It was located to the south of the Imperial City of Luoyang City during the Sui and Tang Dynasties, and aligned with the Yingtian Gate and the Dingding Gate. It was an important part of the central axis of Luoyang City during the Sui and Tang Dynasties, and an important landmark of the urban layout of Luoyang for more than 600 years. This archeological site is located in the river bed about 400 meters west of Luoyang Bridge. The Tianjin Bridge was built in the third year of the reign of Emperor Yang of Sui Dynasty (607 A.D.). It was originally a floating bridge before being destroyed sometime towards the end of the Sui Dynasty. During the time of the Emperor Xuanzong of the Tang Dynasty, the bridge was rebuilt with stone, also known as Luoyang Bridge. There was originally a four-cornered pavilion, railings and pillars on the bridge, and the elegant view of the bridge was famously branded as "Tianjin Bridge and water decorated by moonlight at dawn".

The Hanjia Granary in Luoyang city was built in the Sui Dynasty. It began to store grain on a large scale during the Tang Dynasty and became a major state granary. The granary was 612 meters wide and 710 meters long, covering a total area of 430 thousand square meters. According to relevant historical documents, in the eighth year of Tianbao (749 A.D.) of the Tang Dynasty, the total grain storage of the Hanjia Granary reached 5.8 million units in Dan (a Chinese unit of grains), and was one of the country's large-scale official warehouses. There were special agencies in charge of the administration of this granary and it was guarded by military forces. In a 1972 archeological exploration of the Hanjia Granary, 500 thousand kilograms of carbonized millet was discovered in one of the storage facilities. The grains were still clearly discernible. Inscribed bricks unearthed at the site revealed that the time, amount, breed and source of the grains, the location of the storage facility, the names of the officials who received grain shipments were registered on inscribed bricks kept in the storehouse. Most of the inscribed bricks were produced during

末被毁。唐玄宗时建造为石桥，又称洛阳桥。桥上原有四角亭、栏杆、表柱，清雅幽静的意境使"天津晓月"成为著名的景观。

位于洛阳城区的含嘉仓修建于隋朝，从唐朝开始大规模存粮，成为国家的大型粮仓。粮仓东西宽612米，南北长710米，总面积43万平方米。史载唐天宝八年（公元749年）含嘉仓储粮总量达到580多万石，是全国著名的大型官仓。含嘉仓城设有管理机构，且有驻军守护仓城。1972年含嘉仓遗址考古发掘时，发现在一座仓窖内保存着大约50万斤炭化谷物，颗粒清晰可辨。根据遗址中出土的铭砖可知，粮入窖时，要将储粮的时间、数量、品种、来源、仓窖位置及授领粮食的官员姓名刻于铭砖上，放置于窖中。而铭砖所记大多属于唐高宗、武则天和唐玄宗时期，有调露、天授、长寿和开元等年号。储存的粮食品种有糙米、粟、小豆等。其来源有越州、苏州、徐州、楚州、润州、滁州、随州、魏州、濮州等地。如此广阔的地域范围，如此大的规模，可称之为中国古代最大的粮仓之一。

通济渠荥阳故城段是河南郑州的一段隋唐大运河故道，即今索须河的一段，长18公里，横贯郑州北郊。这段运河早已淤塞，但尚存一座著名的石桥——惠济桥（始建于隋唐，明代重修）。郑州市惠济区有一个村子以此桥为名。惠济桥是一座青石结构、三孔拱券石桥，桥面平铺着平整光滑的青石板。桥面上，两道深深的车辙沟槽十分醒目。

3. 宛洛道

宛洛道是指从洛阳到南阳的道路，这条路从洛阳南下，经平顶山，进入南阳，经唐河、白河到达汉口，与长江相接。道路两旁白河沿岸的新野、南阳市区，唐河沿岸的唐河、赊店、方城等地都成了繁盛的水陆交通枢纽，进而成为南北商品流通的中心。南阳社旗县的赊店镇商业十分繁荣，在民间有"天下店，数赊店""金汉口，银赊店""拉不完的赊店镇"等说法。湖北汉口的货物，由船运到赊店镇上岸，而后再由丝茶商队用牛马骆驼运

the period of Emperor Gaozong, Empress Wu Zetian and Emperor Xuanzong of the Tang Dynasty, according to the reign titles recorded in the inscriptions. The inventory of grains included brown rice, millet, beans and so on. The origins of these grains include Yuezhou, Suzhou, Xuzhou, Chuzhou, Runzhou, Chuzhou, Suizhou, Weizhou and Puzhou. On account of there being so many grain production places, and its super large scale, the Hanjia Granary was the largest grain storage facility in ancient China.

Xingyang old city section of the Tongji Canal, a section of the Sui-Tang Grand Canal in Zhengzhou, which is now a part of Suoxu River, was 18 kilometers long across the northern suburbs of Zhengzhou. The canal has long been silted up, but there still exists a famous stone bridge, the Huiji Bridge (built in the Sui and Tang Dynasties, and reconstructed in the Ming Dynasty). In the Huiji District of Zhengzhou, a village was named after this bridge. Huiji Bridge is a stone-structured, three arched bridge. The bridge deck was paved with smooth bluestone slabs. Viewed from the bridge deck, two deep vehicle ruts are still clearly visible.

3. Wanluo Route

Wanluo Route refers to the part of the Silk Road from Luoyang to Nanyang (referred to as Wan). This route went southward from Luoyang, via Pingdingshan and Nanyang, all the way to Hankou in Hubei Province via the Baihe River and the Tanghe River, and there it connected with the Yangtze River. Adjacent to this route, Xinye County and Nanyang urban areas along the edge of the Baihe River, Tanghe County, Shedian Township and Fangcheng County along the edge of the Tanghe River were prosperous water and land transportation hubs, constituting a cargo distribution center between the north and the south. The Shedian Township of Sheqi County in Nanyang bustled with commercial activities. According to some folk sayings, shops in Shedian were the busiest among their peers, businesses in Shedian were successful next to Hankou, and shops in Shedian were never empty of goods. Goods from Hankou (located in Hubei Province) were transported by ship to Shedian, where caravans picked them up and headed northward along the Silk Road to Mongolia, Russia and Europe.

The Tianfei Temple, the purpose of which was to worship Mazu is still preserved in the urban area of Nanyang. Initially founded between 1662 and 1722 when Emperor Kangxi was in power, this temple served as the shrine of Lin Moniang

载，从这里出发北上，经草原丝绸之路，运抵蒙古、俄罗斯、欧洲。

在南阳市区，至今仍保存着祭祀妈祖的天妃庙。天妃庙建于清朝康熙年间，祭祀着被封为"天妃"的福建女子林默娘，她被尊称为"海洋女神"，是沿海地区行船的渔民和客商的精神寄托。明清时期，白河河宽水大，当时白河码头帆樯林立，客商云集，茶叶、丝绸等货物经汉水、白河船运汇集至南阳，转陆路后再运往各地。随着福建等地客商增多，他们在南阳兴建天妃庙以求河清海晏、舟船平稳，并在每年农历三月廿三、九月初九举行祭礼活动。作为内陆城市，南阳一直保留着供奉海神的妈祖庙，这是很少见的。

4. 太行孔道

太行山陡峭壁立，山西高原和中原内地交通自古就十分不便。为了促进相互间的交流，人们利用太行山山间谷壁，开凿了一系列的山间小路，这些小路被统称为"太行孔道"。河南北上山西的太行孔道主要有：白陉古道、云台古道、羊肠坂古道。

太行八陉之一的白陉位于河南省辉县境内，是山西通往河南的八条最重要的道路之一，长150公里。白陉古道是保存最完整的"悬天古道"，为历朝历代战争调兵运粮和晋豫两省通商、通行的重要通道。

云台古道是一条早已被废弃的古代商道，该条古道北起山西省陵川县，南至河南省辉县，位于云台山风景区中。这条古道修建于宋代，是当时山西通往都城汴梁（今开封）最近的一条大道。古道宽大约3米，青石条铺路。

羊肠坂古道因在山间崎岖缠绕，弯弯曲曲形似羊肠而得名，南起河南沁阳市，北抵山西晋城市，是太行陉最险要的路段。据史料记载，公元前497年，孔子游说赵国，曾过羊肠坡；公元206年，曹操北征叛将高干，路过羊肠坡，适逢大雪，面对军旅生活的艰辛感慨万千，写下著名诗篇《苦

from Fujian Province, who was worshipped as a "Heavenly Princess", a "Goddess of the Sea" and a talisman of fishermen and merchants who sailed in the coastal areas. During the Ming and Qing Dynasties, the Baihe River was wide and abundant with water. At that time, the Baihe Wharf was packed with sail boats. Merchants shipped tea, silk and other goods to Nanyang via the Hanjiang River and Baihe River, transferred them onto land, and finally distributed them to different places. There being more and more merchants from Fujian and other places, they built the Tianfei Temple in Nanyang to pray for good times and held ceremonies on the Chinese lunar calendar March 23 and September 9. It is curiously uncommon that a Mazu temple dedicated to a sea god was established and well preserved in an inland city.

4. The Taihang Tunnel Roads

The Mount Taihang features vertical cliffs and rocky walls. Travelling and transportation between the Central Plains and the Shanxi Plateau used to be a great difficulty. To conquer the difficulty in traversing the mountain, people built roads and trails, some of which were cut along or into the cliff. These paths are collectively and literally referred to as "Taihang Tunnel Roads", of which the closest Chinese equivalent refers to roads built by taking advantage of the natural gaps and openings in the mountain areas. In ancient times, three main tunnel roads went northward from Henan Province to Shanxi Province, including Baixing Path, Yuntai Path and Yangchangban Path.

Baixing Path, one of the eight most important ancient paths built in Mount Taihang and the best-preserved cliff-edge road among the Taihang ancient roads, is located in Huixian County of Henan. 150 kilometers long, this path used to be the most important transport corridor between Henan Province and Shanxi Province. This ancient path has witnessed countless historical moments of ancient military logistic transportation and trade activities between Henan Province and Shanxi Province.

The Yuntai Path was a long-abandoned trade route, of which the location now is in the Yuntai Mountain Scenic Park, between Lingchuan County of Shanxi Province and Huixian County of Henan Province. Built in the Song Dynasty, it was the shortest path between Shanxi and Bianliang (now Kaifeng) the capital city. This ancient road was well-paved with bluestone and about 3 meters wide.

The Yangchangban Path, an awfully zigzagging mountain pathway, the most

寒行》，羊肠坡也由此更名为羊肠坂。

5. 汴洛道

汴洛道也称豫陕官道，西起陕甘，中连汴洛，东至齐鲁。西周灭亡，周朝从长安迁都洛阳，建立东周，郑国从陕西迁到荥阳京襄城，建立东方郑国，都是经由这条官道进出。在唐代，长安和洛阳之间的道路等级最高。到唐德宗时期，开通长安经洛阳至汴州的"大路驿"，由此洛阳和开封之间的道路成为全国等级最高的道路。在中国古代，这条道路是连接东西的交通大动脉，在古代中国的重要性不亚于现在的京港澳高速。沧海桑田，岁月变迁，时光的流逝使汴洛古道的很多路段孤寂无闻，被掩埋于黄土和城市下面。如汴洛古道郑州段部分，就处在今天郑州市区的商都路——郑汴路——东、西大街——中原路之下。

四、联通世界的"一带一路"

2013年9月和10月，中国国家主席习近平分别提出共同建设"丝绸之路经济带"和"21世纪海上丝绸之路"（简称"一带一路"）的合作倡议。"一带一路"倡议很快得到沿线各大经济体的积极响应，自倡议提出以来，合作区域与领域不断拓展，合作模式不断创新完善。

河南省积极参与共建"一带一路"，努力提高对外开放水平，以开放促改革、促发展。河南要建成连通境内外、辐射东中西的国际物流通道枢纽，全力拓展空中、陆上、网上和海上"四条丝路"，为"丝绸之路经济带"建设服务。

difficult one among ancient Mount Taihang Roads. Its name in Chinese means literally "a road on the mountain slope zigzagging like goat guts". The location of this road is between Qinyang County of Henan province and Jincheng County of Shanxi Province. According to relevant historical literature, in Confucius' journey to spread his teachings, he once took this road when he traveled to the Zhao State in 497 B.C. In 206 A.D., the "Three Kingdoms" warlord Cao Cao led an army to fight rebels. He was caught in a heavy snowfall on Yangchangban Path. Feeling emotional about the hardships of military life, Cao wrote a famous poem, *Kuhan Xing (A Rough and Cold Journey)*.

5. The Bianluo Route

The Bianluo (Kaifeng-Luoyang) Route, also known as Yu-Shan State Road, started from Shannxi and Gansu Provinces in the west, ended in Shangdong Province in the east, and connected Kaifeng and Luoyang in the middle. This road witnessed many historic moments, including the cessation of the Western Zhou Dynasty, the relocation of the capital city of Zhou Dynasty from Chang'an to Luoyang to establish the Eastern Zhou Dynasty, and the relocation of Zheng State from Shannxi to the Jingxiang City of Xingyang to establish the Eastern Zheng State. During the Tang Dynasty, the road between Chang'an and Luoyang was well-built. The road from Chang'an via Luoyang to Kaifeng was opened during the reign of the Emperor Dezong of the Tang Dynasty, and it was then the topmost-ranked state road. In ancient China, this road was an east-west artery, which was of no less importance than Beijing-Hong Kong-Macao Expressway is today. Due to the long passage of time, many sections of this ancient thoroughfare were buried under earth and cities were built on top. In Zhengzhou, for instance, right on top of the ancient Bianluo Route lie a chain of modern city roads (Shangdu Road, Zhengbian Road, East Street, West Street and Zhongyuan Road).

IV. The Belt and Road Connecting the World

President Xi Jinping proposed cooperative initiatives to build the Silk Road Economic Belt and the 21st Century Maritime Silk Road in September and October 2013 respectively, which referred to as the Belt and Road Initiative. The initiative quickly received positive responses from major economies along the line. Since its

1. "空中丝绸之路"通达全球

河南的国际航线不断增加,"空中丝绸之路"覆盖圈持续扩大。郑州—卢森堡、郑州—阿姆斯特丹2条航线被纳入中国—欧盟安全智能贸易航线试点计划。河南首条直达欧洲定期客运航线郑州—伦敦航线顺利开航。郑州已开通至温哥华、墨尔本、悉尼、莫斯科、伦敦等5条洲际客运航线,国际客货运航线达到56条(其中客运27条,货运29条),在全球前20位货运枢纽机场中开通16个航点,初步形成了横跨欧美亚三大经济区、覆盖全球主要经济体的国际航线网络。2019年,郑州机场旅客吞吐量约3 000万人次,货邮吞吐量约50万吨。

2. "陆上丝绸之路"纵深发展

中欧班列(郑州)现已初步形成以郑州为枢纽中心的"1+3"国际物流大通道(中欧物流通道和东向亚太、西向中亚、南向东盟通道)、"7个目的站点"和"6个出入境口岸"的通道格局。集货范围覆盖全国四分之三区域,境外网络遍布欧盟及中亚30多个国家与地区的130个城市,境内外合作伙伴达4 000多家,打造出"数字班列""恒温班列"和"运贸一体化"等具有河南特色的班列。2019年,中欧班列(郑州)首条跨境电商专线"菜鸟号"正式开通,这是中国中部地区开通的首条跨境电商商品物流专线。

3. "海上丝绸之路"实现对接

河南省通过铁海联运实现"海上丝绸之路"与"陆上丝绸之路"的对接,建设内陆无水港,开通郑州至连云港、青岛、天津等港口的铁海联运班列,

inception, cooperation areas and fields have continuously expanded. Meanwhile, cooperation models have been increasingly innovated and improved.

Henan Province actively participates in the construction of the Belt and Road and strives to improve the opening up to the outside world. Henan Province is committed to promoting reform and development through opening up. To contribute more to the construction of the Silk Road Economic Belt, Henan will build an international logistics hub which connects China and abroad and radiates to the east, middle and west regions . It will also make all-out efforts to expand the Aerial, Land, Online and Maritime Silk Road as a whole.

1. The expansion of the Aerial Silk Road

Henan's international air routes continue to expand, and the coverage area of the Aerial Silk Road continues to enlarge. The two air routes, Zhengzhou-Luxembourg, Zhengzhou-Amsterdam, have been incorporated into the China-EU Secure and Smart Trade Line Pilot Program (SSTL). Henan's first regular passenger air route to Europe, Zhengzhou-London air route, has been successfully opened. Zhengzhou has opened five intercontinental passenger air routes to Vancouver, Melbourne, Sydney, Moscow and London. International passenger and cargo air routes reach 56 (including 27 passenger air routes and 29 cargo air routes) and 16 destinations in the world's top 20 cargo hub airports have been opened. It thus has formed an initial network of international air routes spanning the three major economic zones of Europe, America and Asia and covering major economies in the world. In 2019, Zhengzhou Airport handled about 30 million passengers and 500,000 tons of cargo and mail.

2. In-Depth Development of the Land Silk Road

China Railway Express (Zhengzhou) has initially formed a corridor structure which consists of "1+3" international logistics corridor with Zhengzhou as the hub (China-Europe logistics corridor and eastbound Asia-Pacific, westbound central Asia and southbound ASEAN corridor), 7 destination stations and 6 entry and exit ports. Its goods collection covers three quarters of China and overseas networks cover 130 cities in more than 30 countries and regions of the European Union and Central Asia. There are more than 4,000 domestic and overseas partners. The trains with Henan's characteristics such as digital trains, constant temperature trains and integration of transportation and trade have been launched . The first cross-border e-commerce special line of China Railway Express (Zhengzhou), which is called

有效连接上海等"海上丝绸之路"重点港口。

4."网上丝绸之路"顺利建设

河南省大力支持跨境电商发展,不断加快E贸易核心功能集聚区规划建设,跨境电商综合试验区综合指标稳居全国第一方阵。2019年,跨境电商零售进出口清单约1亿票,商品总值超过110亿元,居中国中部首位。

"Cainiao", has been officially opened. It is the first cross-border e-commerce special line opened in central China.

3. The Integration of the Maritime Silk Road and the Land Silk Road

Henan Province has connected the Maritime Silk Road and the Land Silk Road through rail-to-sea intermodal transportation and built inland waterless ports. It has opened rail-to-sea intermodal trains from Zhengzhou to such ports as Lianyungang, Qingdao, and Tianjin, thus effectively connecting with key ports of the Maritime Silk Road like Shanghai.

4. The Construction of the Online Silk Road

Henan Province strongly supports the development of cross-border e-commerce and accelerates the planning and construction of e-commerce core functional agglomeration areas. The overall indicators of the cross-border e-commerce enter the first phalanx in China. In 2019, the list of cross-border e-commerce retail imports and exports reached about 100 million times, with a total value of about 11 billion yuan, ranking first in central China.

第二章
物质交流与技术扩散

Chapter II

The Exchange of Goods and Technologies

丝绸之路打通了欧亚大陆两端的世界，并将沿途经过的地区连接起来，成为一条商品、技术和文化的交流带、扩散带。商品贸易是丝绸之路得以形成和持续的推动力，在商品贸易之外，技术和文化的交流传播则推动了欧亚大陆各地的文明发展和生活改善。罗马的玻璃器具，印度的棉织品、香料与宝石是丝路早期输入中国的主要商品，丝绸、瓷器和茶叶是中国输出的主要商品。

河南是丝绸和瓷器的故乡，中国文化的两大象征符号都发源于斯。河洛地区素有"天下之中"的美称，因为交通便利，河东、河北、江淮及湖广的物产汇聚在国际化都市洛阳和开封，呈现在各国客商面前。

一、丝绸的生产和外销

古代西方曾把中国称作"赛里斯"（Seres），Seres是从古希腊语Ser转化而来，也就是"丝国"的意思。"赛里斯"的都城在古罗马文献中被称为"塞拉"（Sera）。中国丝织品在公元前5世纪至公元前6世纪就已经名扬海外，并间接销售到希腊，因此当时的希腊人称中国为"赛里斯"。

有一支古罗马商队在公元100年从马其顿出发前往中国，这支商队所到达的中国都城就是东汉时的洛阳。这是目前被东西方历史文献都证实了的最早的一次古罗马与中国的直接接触。在多数情况下，丝绸是从中国通过安息等地转到欧洲的。

罗马地理学家托勒密的《地理学》中记载了一支马其顿商队从马其顿经过石塔（Lithinos Prygos）到达"赛里斯"首都"塞拉"的故事。中国史书《后汉书》记载："永元十二年（公元100年），冬十一月，西域蒙奇、兜勒二国遣使内附，赐其王金印紫绶。"对比中西史料，大概史实是：大约在公元100年，有一支西方商队从陆路到达中国洛阳，他们来自马其顿。在洛阳，他们受到了东汉政府的热情款待

The communication between Europe and Asia was closely connected with the Silk Road, which made related areas become a platform to exchange commodities and spread technologies and culture. Trade was the driving force for the establishment and the continuation of the Silk Road. Besides, the exchange of technologies and culture promoted civilization and improved people's wellbeing in Europe and Asia. Roman glassware, Indian cotton fabrics, spices and gems, were the main commodities imported into China throughout the early period of the Silk Road, while silk, porcelain and tea were the main commodities exported by China.

Henan was home to silk and porcelain. These two symbols of Chinese culture originated in Henan. The Heluo area is known as the center of the world. Because of the convenient transportation, products from regions like the east and north of the Yellow River, the Yangtze-Huaihe River area, and Hunan and Hubei Provinces, were found in Luoyang and Kaifeng and foreign merchants flocked there for trade.

I. Silk Production and Export

Ancient Western people used to call China "Seres", which stemmed from ancient Greek and meant "silk kingdom". The capital of Seres was called Sera in Roman historical literature. Chinese silk became famous overseas during the 5th and 6th centuries B.C. They were sold indirectly to Greece, hence the Greeks at that time called China Seres.

A Roman caravan left Macedonia for China in 100A.D. They arrived in Luoyang, the then capital of the Eastern Han Dynasty. This was the first direct contact between Rome and China, which was confirmed by western and eastern historical documents. In most cases, silk was exported to Europe via the Parthian Empire and other places.

The Roman geographer Ptolemy's *Geography* recorded that a Macedonian caravan set out from Macedonia via Lithinos Prygos and finally arrived at Sera, the capital of Seres. The Chinese historical book *The Book of the Later Han Dynasty* recorded that two countries in the Western Regions dispatched envoys to Luoyang in November in 100 A.D. The Chinese emperor granted their kings gold seals tied by purple cords. According to historical documents, a conclusion could be drawn to some effect that a western caravan from Macedonia arrived in Luoyang by land

公元166年，一支自称大秦王安敦使节的希腊商团从海路来中国，并到达洛阳，与中央政府商讨中国与地中海建立海上直接贸易联系。这是开辟中国与欧洲直接联系的海上丝绸之路的先声。

河南是桑蚕和丝织业的发源地之一。传说黄帝的妻子嫘祖发明并且传播了养蚕缫丝技术，嫘祖就生活在河南。考古发现也证实在新石器时代河南地区就存在丝织生产，在河南荥阳青台村的仰韶文化遗址中发现了丝织物残片。

汉代中国有两个丝织中心，其中一个就是襄邑（今河南睢县），襄邑是当时中国最主要的织锦产地。在中国丝绸的三大品类（绢、绮、锦）中，锦的制造工艺最为复杂和精巧，因此可以说"襄锦"代表了中国汉代丝织物的最高水平。

由于锦的生产是先将丝进行染色，再用不同颜色的丝通过复杂的方法织成各种图案纹路的织品，其织造难度大，耗费时间多，需要高超的技术，这使襄锦的价格如同黄金一般昂贵，"锦"字就是由金和帛组合而成，表明它是一种贵重如金的丝织品。当时只有襄邑能生产"锦"这种品类的丝绸，所以东汉的文字学家许慎在《说文解字》中，将"锦"字定义为"襄邑织文"（产自襄邑的带有纹饰图案的丝织品）。

由于襄锦品质精美，纹饰华丽，汉代中央政府将襄锦定为皇帝和大臣制作礼服（朝服）的材料，在襄邑设置了叫作"服官"的机构，掌管襄锦的制造，以供应宫廷的衣装。到东汉时期，襄邑民间织锦之风盛行，王充的《论衡》记载："襄邑俗织锦，钝妇无不巧。"就是说襄邑民间妇女一般都会织锦，即使笨拙的妇女，也没有手不巧的。此后直到唐宋时期，襄邑的丝织业都长盛不衰。

从考古发现的资料看，襄邑的丝织品也络绎出现于丝绸之路上。1959年在新疆民丰县一座东汉墓中出土了大批丝织品，其中有3种织有铭文的锦，施染均匀，染色纯正，织造方法复杂，产地应当就是锦的生产中心襄邑。1968年，在新疆吐鲁番阿斯塔那古墓群出土的唐代云头锦鞋，

around the year 100 A.D. They were treated well by the government of the Eastern Han.

In 166 A.D., a group of Greek merchants claiming to be the envoys of Marcus Aurelius came to China by sea and arrived in Luoyang to discuss with the central government about direct trade links between China and the Mediterranean. This was the spearhead of the Maritime Silk Road which connected China directly with Europe.

Henan is a birthplace of sericulture and silk weaving industry. In a legendary story, the Yellow Emperor's wife Madam Lei lived in Henan, and it was she who invented and spread the techniques of raising silkworms and silk reeling. Archaeological findings also confirm that silk making appeared in Henan during the Neolithic Age. This was proven by the discovery of fragments of silk fabrics in the Yangshao Cultural Site of Qingtai Village in Xingyang, Henan Province. (The Yangshao culture was a Neolithic culture that existed extensively along the Yellow River in China.)

During the Han Dynasty, there were two silk weaving centers in China. One of them was Xiangyi (now Sui County, Henan Province, which was the main brocade making place in China at that time. Among the three major categories of Chinese silk (plain woven silk, damask and brocade), brocade's making process is the most complex and exquisite one. Therefore, it can be said that the brocade of Xiangyi represented the finest craftsmanship of Chinese silk fabrics during the Han Dynasty.

During the process of brocade-making, silk was dyed first, and then different colored silk was weaved into fabrics of different patterns by means of complicated weaving methods. It took a long time to weave with great skills, which made it as expensive as gold. The Chinese character "锦"(brocade) is made up of gold and silk, indicating that it is a kind of silk fabric as precious as gold. At that time, silk of this kind could only be produced in Xiangyi. Therefore, Xu Shen, a linguist of the Eastern Han Dynasty, defined "锦" as silk fabrics with decorative patterns produced in Xiangyi in his work *Analytical Dictionary of Characters*.

Due to the exquisite quality and gorgeous patterns of the brocade, the central government of the Han Dynasty designated it to make royal robes for the emperor and his ministers. Consequently, the central government set up an organization to manage brocade making and to supply clothes for the court. During the Eastern Han

鞋面是宝相花平纹经锦，鞋里是花鸟流云纹经锦，这些锦上的花纹图案都是中原地区流行的，织物组织更和汉代的平纹经锦有直接的传承关系。根据丝织物的组织和花纹图案，可以推断丝织物是襄邑所织。这些考古发现反映了襄邑的织锦业持续繁荣，是丝路商旅向欧陆贩运的名贵丝织品。从汉代到唐代，襄邑的织锦一直活跃流通于丝绸之路。

在丝绸之路的西端，欧洲人很早就跨越遥远的距离，接触到了这种昂贵的产品。俄罗斯阿尔泰山北麓的巴泽雷克古墓葬中出土了数量可观的中国丝绣织物。它们带有中国传统的几何纹，有些绣着凤凰飞翔于林间的美丽图案。

中国与中亚的商贸活动在先秦时就有相当规模。1936年，考古学家在阿富汗喀布尔以北约60公里处发掘亚历山大城（约建于公元前4世纪后半叶）时，曾经在一处城堡中发现许多中国的丝织品。月氏人迁居大夏之前，中国的丝织品就已经运往大夏。张骞"凿空"之后，汉代中国与中亚之间的商贸活动越发频繁，经过欧亚大陆各地区的接力，中国丝绸顺畅地到达小亚细亚，再经爱琴海到达希腊。

公元前247年帕提亚人建立的帕提亚帝国（安息帝国），位置正处于中国和欧洲之间，是丝绸之路上重要的中转站。他们有意垄断中国丝绸的运销，阻止中国和希腊、罗马直接交往。公元前53年的卡雷之战，帕提亚王国军队就打着用五颜六色的中国丝绸做的军旗，向入侵的罗马军团进攻，在这场大战中数万罗马士兵毙命。历史学家弗罗鲁斯认为，使罗马军团眼花缭乱的、颜色斑斓的军旗，就是罗马人前所未见的第一批丝绸织物。罗马上层社会非常青睐丝绸，公元前48年恺撒大帝在祝捷会上身穿丝绸服装，带起了一股流行风潮，全罗马的贵族纷纷效仿，罗马甚至出现了专卖丝绸的市场。

不论是西班牙、高卢还是不列颠，凡是罗马帝国统治之处，整个上流社会都热情地追逐着丝绸。英国学者赫德逊在他的《欧洲与中国：从最早时期至1800年的双方关系概述》中描述，安敦尼王朝（96-192）时，

Dynasty, the folk brocade making was prevalent, and Wang Chong's *On Balance* recorded that ordinary women were proficient in brocade weaving in Xiangyi. The silk weaving industry in Xiangyi was prosperous until the Tang and Song Dynasties.

According to archaeological findings, silk fabrics of Xiang Yi were also found on the Silk Road. In 1959, a large number of silk fabrics were unearthed in a tomb of the Eastern Han Dynasty in Minfeng County, Xinjiang Uygur Autonomous Region. Among them there were 3 kinds of brocades with inscriptions, each featuring pure and even in dyeing. Besides, their weaving methods were complicated. It was believed that they were produced in Xiangyi. In 1968, brocade shoes with cloud head were unearthed from the Astana tombs of the Tang Dynasty in Turpan, Xinjiang. There are different patterns on the shoes, the upper is made with warp brocade with lotus flower pattern,the lining is made with warp brocade with flower and bird pattern. These patterns were popular in the Central Plains. The fabric structure was closely connected with that of the Han Dynasty. According to the structure and pattern of the silk fabrics, it can be inferred that the silk fabrics were produced in Xiangyi. These archaeological discoveries prove the continued prosperity of brocade making industry in Xiangyi and show how the precious brocade was transported by merchants along the Silk Road into the European Continent. From the Han Dynasty to the Tang Dynasty, brocade of Xiangyi had a robust circulation on the Silk Road.

At the western end of the Silk Road, Europeans had access to this expensive product that was transported over a long distance. A considerable number of Chinese silk embroidery fabrics were unearthed in the Pazyryk Cemetery at the northern foot of the Altai Mountains of Russia. They had traditional Chinese geometric patterns. Some of them were embroidered with beautiful patterns of a phoenix flying through the forest.

The trade between China and Central Asia was quite frequent in the pre-Qin Period. In 1936, archaeologists excavated Alexandria (established in the late half of the fourth century B.C.) about 60 kilometers north of Kabul, Afghanistan. They found many Chinese silk fabrics in a castle. Before Rouzhi people moved to Tokhgra, Chinese silk fabrics had already been transported there. After the Western Han government dispatched Zhang Qian as an envoy to the Western Regions, the trade between China and Central Asia became more frequent in the Han Dynasty. Through the efforts of various ethnic groups in Eurasia, Chinese silk was introduced

丝织品在罗马帝国极西的伦敦，像在洛阳一样普遍。昂贵的丝绸使罗马的金银不断外流。老普林尼在其《博物志》中估算，这一时期罗马每年支付给阿拉伯半岛、印度和中国的货款就达 1 亿赛斯特提，合 10 万盎司黄金，其中大部分用来购买中国的丝绸。价格等同黄金的中国丝绸，耗尽了罗马的国库。公元 4 年，罗马皇帝迪比琉斯不得不下令禁止男性公民穿丝绸服装。

由于对丝绸的需求量大，丝绸贸易的利润极高，因此养蚕和丝织技术早就开始沿丝绸之路向西传播。在西晋与北朝期间，养蚕技术已经传到丝绸之路上的高昌、于阗等国，丝绸之路上的西域各国有了自己的桑蚕丝织业。

公元 6 世纪，印度修士从西域学习了桑蚕技术，并将蚕种和养蚕技术带到拜占庭。从此以后，丝绸制造业在欧洲建立起来。但是由于一些技术上的不足，拜占庭的养蚕缫丝业无法生产与中国同等质量的优质生丝，再加上桑树种植数量的不足限制了生丝的产量，因此拜占庭仍然要从中国进口大量生丝和丝绸。

二、贵重商品的输入

从汉代开始，中国人就把罗马和波斯看作宝物之乡，认为所有珍稀宝物都来自这里。唐代历史学名著《史记索引》说："珍怪之物，率出大秦。"久而久之，罗马在一些中国人眼中，就成为盛产宝物的圣地。当时中国称罗马为"大秦"，认为罗马人和中国的秦人长相比较接近。《后汉书》写道："其人民皆长大平正，有类中国，故名大秦。"中国人称呼罗马为"大秦"是一种尊重和认可。

最初，西方珠宝进入中原的主要路径是陆上丝绸之路，即经过西亚、中亚、西域诸国输入。而在这条路线上居住的西域人，又常常被中国人称作是"胡人"。在古代中国人看来，胡人因为经常贩卖西方的珍宝，因而也具有特殊的鉴别宝物真假的本领，"胡人识宝"是中国民间故事最重

to Asia Minor, and then reached Greece via the Aegean Sea.

The Parthian Empire, founded by the Parthians in 247 B.C., was situated between China and Europe and later became an important hub on the Silk Road. They intended to monopolize the sale of Chinese silk and prevent direct contacts between China, Greece and Rome. In the Battle of Carrey in 53 B.C., the army of the Parthia Empire attacked the invading Roman armies under colorful Chinese silk flags. In the battle, tens of thousands of Roman soldiers were killed. Historian Florus believed that the dazzling, colorful flags of the Parthian armies were the first silk fabrics ever seen by Romans. Silk was very popular among the upper classes of Rome. In 48 B.C. Caesar dressed in silk clothes at a celebration ceremony, which brought about a fashion trend. All the nobles of Rome followed suit, and there was even a specialized market for silk in Rome.

In Spain, Gaul, Britain and other regions under the rule of Roman Empire, the whole upper class pursued silk passionately. Hudson, an English scholar, described in his book *Europe & China: A Survey of Their Relations from the Earliest Times to 1800* that during the Andonian Dynasty (96 A.D.–192 A.D.), silk in London was as common as that in Luoyang. Rome's gold and silver drained due to the expensive silk. In his *Natural History*, Pliny the Elder estimated that Roman payments to the Arab Peninsula, India and China each year during this period amounted to 100 million Sestertius, or 100,000 ounces of gold, mostly for Chinese silk. Chinese silk, which is priced equal to gold, drained Rome's treasury. In 4 A.D., Tiberius, the Emperor of Rome, had to ban men from wearing silk clothes.

Due to the high demand for silk and extremely high profit of silk trade, sericulture and silk weaving techniques spread west along the Silk Road. During the Western Jin Dynasty and the Northern Dynasties, sericulture technique was transmitted to Qocho, Khotan and other countries on the Silk Road. The western countries on the Silk Road had their own sericulture industry.

In the 6th century, Indian monks learned sericulture technique from the Western Regions and brought silkworm eggs and rearing techniques to Byzantium. Since then, silk weaving industry was established in Europe. However, due to some technical deficiencies, the Byzantine silk reeling industry could not produce raw silk of the same quality as that of Chinese silk. In addition, insufficient mulberry planting curbed the production of raw silk. As a result, Byzantine still imported a large

要的题材之一。这类故事最早出现于中国的魏晋时期，在唐代最为流行，此后逐渐消失。到了明代，故事里的胡人已经不再来自西域陆路，而是来自海上。

这些故事的背后，反映的是真实的中西贸易史。当时中西方的陆路交通远远无法与现代相比，人们面对一些来自异域的稀缺商品，充满了不可抑制的好奇心。在利益的驱使下，商人们甘愿冒着风险，付出巨大代价，通过陆路进行长途运输。根据中国历史书籍的记载，通过丝绸之路进入中原的贵重商品主要有：品类繁多的宝石、金银器、玻璃、罗马的杂色绫、火浣布、波斯、阿拉伯的棉织品、毛织品，特别是各种地毯、壁毡、毛毯等。

在公元18世纪以前，太平洋的珊瑚还没有得到开发，世界上唯一的珊瑚产地就是地中海沿岸，中国古代使用的所有宝石珊瑚都来自古罗马属地。在中国河南，有一个家喻户晓的故事——石崇斗富，它可以说明当时中国富裕阶层对西方宝石的看重和庞大的需求。

在晋朝的京都洛阳，有三个出名的大富豪：一个是掌管禁军的羊琇，一个是晋武帝的舅父王恺，还有一个是高官石崇。石崇热衷于炫耀财富。王恺作为大富豪，也不甘寂寞，两人经常比赛炫富。有一次，王恺比赛失利，向晋武帝求援，晋武帝遂将国库里的宝物——一株二尺高的珊瑚送给他，希望压倒石崇。王恺向石崇炫耀这株珊瑚，谁知道石崇挥起铁如意，把它砸得粉碎。面对大惊失色的王恺，石崇从容地说："我家有的是珊瑚，随便赔你一株好了。"果然，在石崇的宝库里，王恺见到了几十株珊瑚树。每一株都高大挺秀，晶莹剔透，比起王恺的那株，其色彩和质地要胜过几倍。王恺这才明白，自己家的财宝确实比不过他，只好认输作罢。

在这个故事中，石崇的行为揭示了古代中国一些富裕阶层的奢侈生活，像珊瑚这样珍贵的稀缺物品，他们不仅不珍惜和欣赏，反而把它们变成炫耀自己财富的工具。在现代人看来，这些行为当然是不恰当的。但是，这个故事中关于珊瑚的描述说明，当时的河南与古罗马已经有相当频繁的商贸联系。

quantity of raw silk from China.

II. Introduction of Valuable Commodities

Since the Han Dynasty, Chinese people had regarded Rome and Persia as the home of treasures, and believed that all rare treasures came from there. The famous historical book *Historical Index* of the Tang Dynasty said that treasures all originated from Da Qin. As time passed, Rome became a holy place full of treasures in the minds of some Chinese people. At that time, China called Rome Da Qin and believed that the Romans looked like the Chinese of the Qin Dynasty. *The Book of the Later Han* wrote, "The people are all tall and good looking just like Chinese people, so the country was called Da Qin." To some extent, Chinese people called Rome Da Qin out of a kind of respect and recognition.

Initially, Western jewelry was transported to the Central Plains mainly through the Silk Road on the land. They were introduced through the countries of West Asia, Central Asia and the Western Regions. The Westerners who lived along this route were often referred as "Hu people". In the eyes of the ancient Chinese people, Hu people had a special ability to identify genuine or fake treasures because they often sold the treasures of the West. "Hu People's identifying treasures" is one of the most important subjects of Chinese folktales. This kind of story first appeared in the Wei and Jin Dynasties and peaked during the Tang Dynasty. Later, such kinds of story disappeared. During the Ming Dynasty, the Hu people in the story no longer came from the Western Regions by land, but by sea.

These stories reflect a true history of Sino-Western trade. At that time, the transportation on land between China and the West was backward in contrast to that of modern times. People had a strong desire to obtain rare goods from foreign countries. Driven by making profits, the merchants were willing to take risks and paid a huge price to transport them by land. According to the records of Chinese history books, the precious goods that were transported to the Central Plains through the Silk Road mainly included a wide variety of precious stones, gold vessels and silver wares, glass, Roman motley twill damask, asbestos cloth, Persian and Arabic cotton and wool products including carpets, wall mats, blankets, etc.

Before the 18th century, Pacific coral had not been exploited and the coral in the

除了珊瑚，从西域传入中原的金银器品类也很多，并深受中原人的喜爱。文献资料和考古发现都证实，伊朗地区发达的金器制作工艺沿着陆上丝绸之路传到了中国。中国本土出现金银器皿的时代并不晚，只是比起同时代的欧洲、西亚和中亚，古代中国的金银器制作技术还不够发达。随着张骞出使西域，中西之间的往来通道被疏通了，商旅和使节纷纷将精美的金银器带到中国。中国多地发现的西汉初期贵族墓葬，都有波斯风格的银器出土，很可能是同一批产品被皇室获得，后分赐给了贵族。到了唐代，金银器皿在中国的使用越发普遍，皇室贵族大量使用金银制作生活器具和佛教器具。唐代金银器普遍借鉴波斯、中亚等地的风格，并且和中国传统的器具类型、装饰图案相融合，形成了一种中西合璧、雍容华贵的艺术风格。

河南洛阳出土过一件八棱带把的银杯，装饰精细丰富，整体外观大气华贵，带有浓郁的中亚色彩。除了来自中亚的银器，洛阳地区墓葬中还出土过大量的罗马风格的器物，其中比较典型的金银器有高足杯、多曲长杯等。高足杯最早出现于罗马帝国统治下的地中海地区，其后经过中亚传入中国。洛阳博物馆收藏了一件洛阳出土的高足银杯，其基本特征为：平底、高足、折腹，高足上有托盘，足为花瓣形，中间有算盘珠节，是典型的罗马风格银杯。北京大学赛克勒考古与艺术博物馆收藏了一件高足杯，杯体纹饰为三层，上层和下层分别是缠枝纹，中层为狩猎纹，刻画了四名猎手捕猎的情景。该杯出土于洛阳北部的邙山，有折腹、算盘珠节、高足托盘等三个罗马风格的基本要素。此外，1981年在洛阳市伊川县水寨乡，1984年在洛阳市宜阳县张坞乡，都曾出土过制作精美的具有异域风情的高足银杯。这些银杯的出现，表明带有中亚和罗马风格的金银器产品在古代河南人的生活中已经相当普遍。

另外一种金银器叫作多曲长杯，这种器物在波斯曾经非常流行，后来逐渐传到中亚，并最终传入唐代中国。多曲长杯一般呈椭圆形，杯腹较浅。1991年，在洛阳市伊川县鸦岭乡的唐齐国太夫人墓中，出土了两件四曲金长杯（图2-1），内有突棱、圈足，底部中心有双鱼环绕。这是波斯风

world originated exclusively from the Mediterranean coast at that time. All the coral used in ancient China came from Roman territories. In Henan, there is a household story of "Competition in Wealth", which can be used to explain the strong desire and huge demand for western gems in the wealthy classes of China.

In Luoyang, the capital of the Jin Dynasty, there were three famous rich figures. One was Yang Xiu, who was in charge of the imperial guards, the second was Wang Kai, who was the uncle of Emperor Wu of the Jin Dynasty and the third was Shi Chong, who was a high official. Shi Chong liked to flaunt his wealth to show his pride and chivalry, and so did Wang Kai. These two often competed in showing off their wealth. On one occasion, Wang Kai lost the competition and asked Emperor Wu of the Jin Dynasty for help. The Emperor gave him a treasure from the national treasury, a two-foot-high coral, hoping to defeat Shi Chong. Wang Kai demonstrated the coral to Shi Chong. Surprisingly, Shi Chong broke it into pieces with an iron ruyi. Seeing this, Wang Kai was greatly shocked while Shi Chong calmly said that he had some coral trees in his home and any one of them could be used to compensate for the broken one. As expected, Wang Kai saw dozens of coral trees in the house of Shi Chong. The trees were tall and beautiful, glittering and translucent. Compared with Wang Kai's coral, they were more exquisite in color and quality. Only then did Wang Kai realize that the treasure of his own was no match to Shi Chong's, so he had to give up and threw in the towel.

In this story, Shi Chong's behavior indicated the luxurious life of the affluent classes of ancient China. They didn't cherish or enjoy such precious and scarce commodities as coral, but used them to show off their wealth. Such behavior is, of course, inappropriate for modern people. However, the description of coral in this story also suggested that Henan and ancient Rome at that time had frequent commercial links.

In addition to the coral, there were many gold vessels and silverware introduced into the Central Plains from the Western Regions and they were deeply loved by the people. Both the literature and archaeological findings confirm that the advanced techniques of goldware making in Iran were introduced to China through the Silk Road. The time when gold and silver utensils appeared in China was not too late, but compared to contemporary Europe, West Asia and Central Asia, gold and silver utensils making techniques in ancient China were still backward. After the Western Han government

图2-1 伊川县唐墓出土四曲双鱼纹长杯

Fig.2-1 An oblong cup with double fish unearthed from a tomb of the Tang Dynasty in Yichuan County

格影响中原器物的又一个直接的例子。

除了金银器之外，伊朗发明的锌铜合金——在中国被称为"黄铜"，也作为一种贵重金属传入中国。早在隋朝，中国已经有了从萨珊王朝进口黄铜的记录，一般用其来制作饰品或佛像。到了元明时期，冶炼黄铜的技术在中国已经比较普及。当然，商品和技术的传播是双向的：如有一些胡商，就从河南洛阳搜寻金银制品带回中亚；又如提炼金属锌的技术，一般认为是在公元16世纪从中国传入了欧洲。

玻璃也是经丝绸之路输入中原的一种稀缺商品。透明或半透明的玻璃制品，因为它们在古代社会的稀缺性，以及其晶莹剔透的外观，在中国常常被看作是一种奢侈的宝石，宋代以前玻璃的市场价格甚至高于金银。河南洛阳中州路的西周墓葬出土过一些半透明的圆珠、管珠等，是含有少量玻璃的多晶石英珠，可以看作是中国早期的原始玻璃制品。这类珠子在全国各地西周墓葬中屡有发现，表明西周时期的中国人可能已经掌握了制作玻璃的基本技术。从战国至汉代，中原人常使用一种名叫"蜻蜓眼玻

dispatched Zhang Qian as an envoy to the Western Regions, the communication between China and the West increased. Merchants, travelers and envoys brought beautiful gold vessels and silverware to China. In many parts of China, Persian-style silverware was unearthed in the tombs of the nobles of the early Western Han Dynasty. It is likely that the same batch of products were obtained by the royal family and later bestowed upon these nobles. During the Tang Dynasty, the use of gold and silver utensils in China became more prevalent. The royal family used lots of gold and silver to make utensils for daily use and Buddhist activities. The gold and silver utensils of the Tang Dynasty generally borrowed the styles of Persia and Central Asia, and they were integrated with traditional Chinese utensils and decorative patterns to form an elegant artistic style that reflects a good combination of Chinese and Western culture.

An octagonal cup with a handle was unearthed in Luoyang. Its ornamentation is exquisite and luxurious with strong Central Asian characteristics. In addition to the silverware from Central Asia, a large number of Roman-style artifacts were unearthed from the tombs of Luoyang, among which are gold and silverware of this kind including stem cups and oblong cups. The stem cups first appeared in the Mediterranean region under the rule of the Roman Empire. They were later introduced to China through Central Asia. Luoyang Museum has a silver bead-stem cup unearthed in Luoyang, with a flat bottom, a stem and a folded belly. Besides this, there is a tray in a petal shape on the stem. It is a typical Roman-style silver cup. The Arthur M. Sackler Museum of Art and Archaeology at Peking University has a stem cup. Its ornamentation is divided into three parts: the upper and lower parts are interlaced floral patterns, and the middle part is hunting patterns about four hunters' hunting. The cup was unearthed in the Mount Mang in the north of Luoyang. It has three basic elements of Roman style, namely a folded belly, a bead, and a stem tray. In addition, exquisite silver stem cups with exotic styles were unearthed in Shuizhai Township, Yichuan County of Luoyang in 1981 and in Zhangwu Township, Yiyang County of Luoyang in 1984 respectively. These silver cups show that gold and silver products with Central Asian and Roman styles were available to the people of ancient Henan.

Another kind of utensil is called an oblong cup. This kind of utensil was very popular in Persia, and it was introduced to Central Asia later, and finally to China in the Tang Dynasty. The cup is generally elliptical with shallow bellies. In 1991, two gold oblong cups (fig. 2−1) were unearthed in the Tang tomb of Mrs. Qi Guotai in

璃珠"的饰品，类似之物早在公元前 15 世纪就出现于美索不达米亚和埃及。公元前 13 世纪，蜻蜓眼玻璃珠已经广泛流行于中亚、西亚。从时间顺序上看，中国的玻璃制作技术可能受到了西方技术的影响。但是现代化学检测表明，中国出土的玻璃珠有自身的独特性，其制成品绚丽多彩，但易碎、不耐高温、透明度差，不适应骤冷骤热的环境条件。一般认为，从外国输入的玻璃珠皆为钠钙玻璃，而铅钡玻璃则是中国自身的发明，两者外观虽然相近，却属于两种不同的制作技术体系。

但是，由于中国本土玻璃技术发展的不足，生产的玻璃器具在实用方面还难以满足需要，所以人们对来自西方的更加精致的玻璃制品就非常推崇和喜爱。研究表明，目前中国已经发现的早期玻璃制品，外国进口的数量远超中国自产。在地中海沿岸，罗马人很早就开始生产玻璃，自公元前 4 世纪起，他们的玻璃产品就已经远销世界各地。汉代以后，中国出现了盘、碗、瓶、杯等各种玻璃容器，它们有些是用中国本土的铅钡玻璃制作的，也有一些是从地中海传来的罗马产品。例如，河南省洛阳市东郊东汉墓出土的玻璃瓶（图 2-2），就是一件著名的罗马玻璃器具，它采用模压、吹制成型技法，工艺迥异于中国。在中国历史上，一些文献在提到玻璃的时候，会使用"琉璃""璧琉璃""颇黎"等种种带着异域色彩的别名，说明这种产品一般都与罗马帝国有不可分割的渊源。

继罗马之后，波斯的玻璃生产技术又在西方世界兴起。波斯人擅长在玻璃器物表面，用勾挑和磨琢的工艺制造乳钉或凹凸圆形的装饰。这类器物在中国的新疆、宁夏、陕西、北京、河南、湖北等地都有出土。1971 年河南省洛阳市关林出土过一件素面玻璃瓶，瓶高 11 厘米，器身直径却有 11.5 厘米，器身呈圆球形，透明，圆唇、小口、细颈，整体呈翠绿色，其形状和工艺与伊朗出土的玻璃器物相似，据推测是波斯人制作的香水瓶。加拿大皇家安大略博物馆也收藏了一件类似的玻璃瓶，是出土于洛阳唐墓，后流失到海外的珍贵藏品。

到了中国唐代，伊斯兰玻璃手工业兴起，取代波斯产品输入中国。

Yaling Township, Yichuan County. They have ribs and round feet, and the center of the bottom is surrounded by two fish. This is another typical example to show that the Persian style affected artifacts of the Central Plains.

In addition to gold and silver utensils, the zinc-copper alloy invented by Iran, which is called brass in China, was also introduced to China as a precious metal. As early as the Sui Dynasty, China had a record of importing brass from the Sassanid Empire, and it was generally used to make ornaments or Buddha statues. During the Yuan and Ming Dynasties, the technology of smelting brass was popularized in China. Surely, the spread of goods and technologies was a two-way process. For example, some Hu merchants purchased gold and silver products in Luoyang and took them back to Central Asia. Another example is the technology of refining zinc, which is generally believed to have been introduced to Europe from China in the 16th century.

Glass was also a scarce commodity that was imported into the Central Plains through the Silk Road. Transparent or translucent glass products were often seen as luxury gems in China because of their scarcity in ancient society and their crystal-clear appearance. Before the Song Dynasty, the price of glass was even higher than gold and silver in the markets. Some translucent round and tube beads were excavated from the Western Zhou Tombs near Zhongzhou Road, Luoyang city. These are polycrystalline quartz beads containing a small amount of glass, which can be regarded as the original glass products of early China. These kinds of beads are frequently found in the tombs of the Western Zhou Dynasty throughout China, indicating that Chinese people of the Western Zhou Dynasty had the basic technology of making glass. From the Warring States to the Han Dynasty, people of the Central Plains often used dragonfly-eye glass beads as accessories. Similar products appeared in Mesopotamia and Egypt as early as the 15th century B.C. In the 13th century B.C., such glass beads were widely used in Central Asia and West Asia. In terms of chronological order, China's glass making technology might have been affected by Western technology. Modern chemical tests have shown that the glass beads unearthed in China had a peculiarity. They are colorful but fragile. They are not resistant to high temperature, not very transparent, and not suitable for sudden cooling and heating, etc. It is generally believed that glass beads imported from foreign countries are soda-lime glass, while lead-barium glass was invented by China itself. Although their appearances are similar, they fall into two different making systems.

However, due to the inadequate development of glass technology in China,

图2-2 洛阳东汉墓出土的玻璃瓶　摄影：何迎涛
Fig. 2-2 A glass bottle unearthed from a tomb of the Eastern Han Dynasty in Luoyang

伊斯兰玻璃器皿采用吹制成型技法，纹样以几何、花卉刻纹为主，有其自身的一些特性。总之，丝绸之路沿线各国密切的商贸联系，让中国进口玻璃制品的过程和西方玻璃发展的历史基本同步。

以珊瑚、金银器、玻璃等种种珍宝为代表，西域商人的活动不仅给中原人民带来了异域的贵重商品，而且还带来很多实用的生活用品，比如胡床、胡帐和榻。这些方便实用的家具，首先在洛阳流行开来，然后推广到全国。它们大大改变了中国人的生活方式。

劝君莫惜金缕衣，劝君惜取少年时。

花开堪折直须折，莫待无花空折枝。

这是一首唐诗。所谓"金缕衣"，是指专门在跳舞时穿着的华丽服装。

glassware could not meet the demands for practical use. Consequently, people were keen on exquisite glass products from the West. Studies suggest that the amount of imported glass is far higher than that of made in China. Along the Mediterranean coast, the Romans began to produce glass quite early. Since the 4th century B.C., their glass products had been exported to all parts of the world. After the Han Dynasty, a variety of glass containers like plates, bowls, bottles, and cups appeared in China. Some of them were made by Chinese people with lead-barium glass, and some were Roman products introduced from Mediterranean areas. For example, the famous glass bottle (fig. 2−2) unearthed from the Tomb of the Eastern Han Dynasty in the eastern suburbs of Luoyang City, Henan Province. It is a Roman style bottle made with mold-blown glass making technique, which is different from that in China at the time. In the history of China, people used exotic names to refer to glass in some documents, indicating that glass utensils had an inseparable connection with the Roman Empire.

The Persian technology of glass production sprang up in the Western world after Rome's. The Persians were good at making nipple nails or concave-convex ornaments on glassware surfaces by grinding and other skills. This kind of glassware was unearthed in Xinjiang, Ningxia, Shaanxi, Beijing, Henan, Hubei and other places in China. In 1971, a plain glass bottle, 11 cm high and 11.5 cm in diameter, was unearthed in Guanlin, Luoyang. The body is round, transparent and emerald green with a round lip, small mouth, and narrow neck. Its shape and craft are similar to that of glass bottle excavated in Iran. It is presumed that it is a perfume bottle made by Persians. The Royal Ontario Museum also has a similar glass bottle, which was unearthed from the tomb of the Tang Dynasty in Luoyang and then looted overseas.

During the Tang Dynasty, the Islamic glass handicraft industry boomed and was introduced to China, so Persian glass products were replaced by Islamic ones. Islamic glassware adopted the mold-blown technique, and the pattern was mainly composed of geometric and floral engraving with its own characteristics. In short, the close trade links of countries along the Silk Road made the process of China's importing glass products basically in sync with the development of western glass.

The commercial activities of merchants from the Western Regions not only brought valuable commodities such as coral, gold utensils and silverware, glassware to the people of the Central Plains, but also brought many practical daily necessities, such as beds, tents and couches. This convenient and practical furniture first became

唐代宫廷歌舞受中亚影响很深，所以当时的舞衣往往也带有西域特色。根据汉、唐两代史书记载，西域各国擅长制造掺杂金线的织物，这类织物深受中国古代宫廷喜爱，常被买来用作后妃的衣料。另外，毛纺织技术是古代中国发展较为薄弱的一个领域，西域地区生产的棉、毛织物很受欢迎。中国出土的毛织物图案题材明显受西方影响，常见的连珠纹、孔雀、狮子、骆驼、翼马、胡商、骑士等纹样都来自西亚。

三、生物品种的交流

河南人喜欢以烩面（图2-3）为代表的面食。在很多"老河南"看来，面条是最美味也最容易消化的食品。在世界的任何角落，烩面总能唤起河南游子埋藏在心底的乡情。河南烩面代表了古老中州的朴实，洁白宽厚的面片，浓香稠厚的羊肉汤，洒上芫荽，浇上辣椒油，鲜美无比，勾人食欲。这一碗乡土风味的烩面，追根到底还是丝绸之路带给河南的馈赠。

烩面的首要特点，在于使用羊肉汤（或牛肉汤）来烹煮小麦做成的

图2-3 河南烩面（张勋，王爽秋供图）
Fig. 2-3 Huimian(Henan stewed noodles)

popular in Luoyang, and then spread all over China. They greatly changed the way of life of Chinese people.

"I'd like to discourage you from indulging in your robes made of golden threads, I'd like to encourage you to cherish and honor your youthful days. Make your picking when flowers are in bloom. Wait not till out of bloom to pick on twigs and sprigs in vain." This is a popular song from the Tang Dynasty. The so-called "golden dress" refers to the gorgeous costumes specially worn when dancing. The court songs and dances during the Tang Dynasty were deeply influenced by Central Asia, so the dancing clothes often had some features of the Western Regions. According to the historical records of the Han and Tang Dynasties, people of the Western Regions were good at making fabrics with gold threads. These fabrics were deeply loved by the imperial court of ancient China and were often bought as clothes for empresses. Besides, wool textile technology was relatively backward in ancient China, so the cotton and wool fabrics produced in the Western Regions were very popular among Chinese People. The patterns of the wool fabrics unearthed in China were obviously influenced by the West. The common patterns, such as joint-beads, peacocks, lions, camels, winged horses, Hu merchants and knights, all came from West Asia.

III. Communication of Biological Species

People in Henan prefer noodles, especially Huimian (Henan stewed noodles) (fig.2–3). For many natives of Henan, noodles are a delicious and digestible food. In any corner of the world, a bowl of Huimian can always arouse Henan travelers' homesickness buried deep in their hearts. Huimian of Henan represents the simplicity of ancient Henan. White and wide noodle sheets were put into thick and fragrant mutton soup in a bowl with coriander and chili oil. Such stewed noodles are delicious and appetizing. This bowl of noodles with local flavor is a gift for Henan brought by the Silk Road.

Henan stewed noodles are featured by using mutton soup (or beef soup) to cook noodles made from wheat. The combination of noodles and mutton easily arouses the association of the Silk Road. Pasta was popular in West and Central Asia. Wheat, a crop native to West Asia, was widely introduced to Europe and Asia in prehistoric times. The Chinese diet was greatly influenced by travelers on the Silk Road, making

面条。面和羊肉的搭配，非常容易激起有关丝绸之路的联想。丝绸之路经行的西亚、中亚普遍流行面食。小麦这种农作物原产于西亚，史前时代就已经在欧亚大陆广泛传播。丝路来客带给中国饮食的影响，也以面食为主。从汉代到唐宋，牛、羊、猪肉是中国人经常食用的肉类品种，其中牛肉最受欢迎。但是，中国古代农业主要使用牛耕，为了保护珍贵的畜力，政府往往有严格的规定，禁止宰杀耕牛，所以中国人日常食用的肉类，上层社会以羊肉为主，中下层人民则多食猪肉。遗憾的是，中原农耕地区密集饲养得到的羊肉比较膻，口感明显不如西北游牧地区的羊肉，所以中原人就喜欢通过商人从西域购入羊肉。后来，当伊斯兰教在中亚广泛传播以后，西域来客对于羊肉的喜爱和食用，也影响了中原人的饮食偏好。

烩面中常见的配菜，不少也是通过丝绸之路被中原人认识和食用的。烩面的重要配菜芫荽，原名胡荽，相传是在张骞通西域时传入中国。烩面的主要调味料是胡椒和辣椒。胡椒原产于印度，后引种到波斯，又沿丝路进入中国；辣椒则是从海上传入中国的南美植物。总而言之，河南人爱吃的烩面，它的食材和调料大部分都是来自丝绸之路上的异域生物制品。与此同时，它们在河南这块开放的土地上实现了与当地食物的融合。

在丝绸之路形成以前，小麦、大麦的种植技术都已经传入中国。但是，在种植小麦之初，古代中国人不会磨制面粉，所以主要采用"粒食"的办法，老百姓也因此而被称作"粒食之民"。"粒食"的麦子常常带有外壳，这样的口感显然不能让人满意，所以中国北方主要还是种植本土物种粟。1956年，考古工作者在洛阳发现了战国时代的石磨，证明中国大约在战国时期已经拥有了比较成熟的磨面技术。大约到了东汉中期，中国人又掌握了比较成熟的发酵技术。这样，高质量、多品种的面食在河南才具备了食用和推广的条件。河南面食中有一个重要品种被称为"饼"：烤熟来吃的叫"烧饼"，蒸熟的叫"蒸饼"，煮熟的叫"汤饼"。汉唐时期，河南等地非常流行一种叫作"胡饼"的食物，取名"胡饼"，一来是因为这种食品来自西域，二来也是因为饼上撒着喷香的芝麻——当时称作胡麻。

noodles the staple food in China. From the Han Dynasty to the Tang and Song Dynasties, beef, mutton and pork were the most common meat for Chinese people, and beef was the most popular one. However, cows were mainly used to plough the land in ancient China. In order to protect this animal power, the government tended to ban the slaughtering of cows. Therefore, the upper class took mutton as the main meat for daily consumption, while the lower and middle classes mainly ate pork. Unfortunately, the mutton produced in the Central Plains has a heavy smell and tastes much worse than that produced in the nomadic areas of the northwest region, so people in the Central Plains preferred to buy mutton from the Western Regions through merchants. Later, after Islam was widely spread through Central Asia, visitors from the Western Regions preferred mutton. To some extent, it also affected the dietary preferences of people in the Central Plains.

Many common ingredients in Henan stewed noodles were also known and eaten by people in the Central Plains through the Silk Road. One important ingredient of Henan stewed noodles is coriander, which is called Hu coriander originally. It is said that coriander was introduced to China during the time when the Western Han government dispatched Zhang Qian as an envoy to the Western Regions. The main seasoning for Henan stewed noodles includes pepper and chili pepper. Pepper was native to India, and was introduced to Persia and then to China along the Silk Road. Chili pepper was a South American plant and it was introduced to China by sea. All in all, the main ingredients and seasonings of Henan stewed noodles are exotic biological products from the Silk Road. Meanwhile, they are integrated with local food in Henan.

Before the formation of the Silk Road, the cultivation techniques of wheat and barley had been introduced to China. However, in the early days of the cultivation of wheat, Chinese people did not know how to grind the wheat into flour, thus they ate it without deep processing, Therefore, Chinese common people were also called "grain-eating people". People ate wheat with shells, so it was not tasty. Hence, people in northern China mainly grew native species—millet. In 1956, archaeologists discovered a stone mill of the Warring States Period in Luoyang, which proved that China had a relatively mature grinding technique during the Warring States Period. In the middle of the Eastern Han Dynasty, Chinese people mastered mature fermentation technology. In this way, varieties of food made of flour was consumed and promoted in Henan. An important variety of Henan pasta was called Bing

美国东方学者、人类学家劳费尔早在 1919 年就写成他的名著《中国伊朗编》，书中列举了多种从伊朗传入中原的植物。反过来，中国本土植物外传，也对世界产生了重要影响，其中粮食作物的影响最大。上古之时，中国比较重要的粮食品种有水稻、粟、大豆、菰米和大麻籽。其中菰米和大麻籽产量过低，早已不作粮食使用，水稻、粟和大豆作为中国本土植物，一直是中国重要的粮食作物。

粟是商朝的主要农作物。商周以后，粟仍是黄河流域占据首位的粮食作物。粟在中唐之前一直是河南地区最重要的粮食作物，被称为"五谷之首"。

据考证，粟可能是由中国西南地区的商人通过陆路经缅甸、泰国和马来半岛而传入南洋群岛。早在公元前 1700 年，法国的阿尔卑斯地区就开始了粟的引种栽培。粟在大移民时代由欧洲人带入美国，19 世纪中叶后，由于奖励政策，粟的传播和种植进入新阶段，20 世纪初已占美国黍类作物的 90%。

在中世纪的欧洲，粟被广泛种植，它是当时穷人最依赖的食物。到了 19 世纪，小麦、马铃薯、玉米、黑麦和水稻等农作物种植面积扩大，这些粮食作物的高产属性以及人们饮食习惯的改变导致粟的地位有所下降，这与相同历史时期中国北方粟地位之下降的原因相类似。今天粟依然在欧洲西部的一些地区种植，其用途略有变化，主要作为家畜饲料。而在欧洲的东部地区，粟一直作为面包和发酵酒的重要原料，仍然具有举足轻重的地位。

粟的西传路线，研究者认为有两条：一是地中海方向，具体传播路线为希腊到南斯拉夫、意大利、法国南部的普罗旺斯、西班牙；二是多瑙河流域方向，具体传播路线为东南欧、中欧、荷兰、比利时等国家和地区。粟的传播开创了欧洲原始农业的先河。

粟在东亚的传播主要是通过山东半岛或辽东半岛，传入朝鲜和日本等国家。日本在绳文时代末期已经栽培粟，引入水稻后，粟的种植面积有

(a kind of pancake): it was called Shaobing (baked bread pancake) when cooked, Zhengbing (steamed pancake) when steamed, and Tangbing (boiled pancake) when boiled. During the Han and Tang Dynasties, a kind of food called "Hu pancake" was popular in Henan and other places. The name of "Hu pancake" suggested that it came from the Western Regions, and it was sprinkled with sesame seeds (sesame was called Hu sesame then).

Berthold Laufer, an American orientalist and anthropologist, wrote a famous book *Sino-Iranica* in 1919, in which he listed a variety of plants that were introduced into the Central Plains from Iran. In turn, the spread of Chinese native plants also greatly influenced the world. Among them, food crops played a big role. In ancient times, rice, millet, soybean, wild rice and hemp seeds were relatively important food crops in China. Wild rice and hemp seeds were no longer food crops due to their low production, while rice, millet and soybean, as native plants of China, have always been important food crops in China.

Millet was the main crop in the Shang Dynasty. After the Shang and Zhou Dynasties, millet was still the most important food crop in the Yellow River Basin. Before the Middle Tang Dynasty, millet had been the most important food crop in Henan. It was called the "first of the grain".

It was likely that millet was introduced to the South Sea Islands by merchants from Sichuan and Yunnan via the land routes of Myanmar, Thailand and the Malay Peninsula. As early as 1700 B.C., millet was introduced and cultivated in the French Alps. In the era of immigration, millet was introduced to the United States by Europeans. After the 1950s it entered a new stage due to incentive policies. At the beginning of the 20th century, it accounted for 90% of all US millet crops.

In medieval Europe, millet was of vital importance for the poor. By the 19th century, wheat, potato, corn, rye, and rice were widely grown. This was attributed to the high yield of these food crops and changes in eating habits, which was similar to that in northern China during the same historical period, where millet became less important than before. Up until now, millet has been cultivated in certain places for animal feeds in Western Europe, while millet has always been an important raw material for bread and fermented wine in Eastern Europe.

Some researchers believe that the westward route of millet via West Asia can be divided into two channels of communication: the first is the channel along the

所下降。也可以说，在史前至迟到中古时期，粟的种植范围已经扩散到当时世界上已知的大部分地区。

粟具有较强的抗逆性，价格低廉，这决定了它可以种植在相对贫瘠的土地上，且能在年景相对不好的时候取得产量并用于救荒。粟在世界古代史、中古史上具有不可或缺的食用价值。罗马帝国把粟作为重要作物，贯穿农业社会的始终，粟对其经济发展、文化繁荣等都起了一定的促进作用。

河南是大豆的主要原产地。大豆是河南人从古至今极宝贵的农业资源，也是营养丰富的粮油、饲料兼优的农作物。大豆从河南走向世界的时间晚于粟，所以时间脉络清晰。公元前3000年，河南大豆开始传入日本，2000年后传入朝鲜。在汉代之前，中国南方地区尚不知大豆，所以亚洲南部地区，均是在1世纪到地理大发现的15世纪之间推广的大豆，至迟在13世纪传入印度尼西亚等东南亚地区。从1740年至1879年的一百多年间，大豆从欧洲传入美洲、非洲、大洋洲等地区。

四、医药、天文历法的交流

1. 医学交流

丝绸之路的开通不仅使东西方之间的物品交流更加便捷，也促进了医药技术的交流。早在唐朝以前，印度的医学就已经对中国的医学产生了重要影响，许多印度医学著作，尤其是佛教的医典都被翻译成了中文。到唐朝时，印度医学著作的影响进一步加深，具有特殊效验的眼科是印度医学对唐朝医学产生影响的一个重要领域。王焘撰成于唐天宝十一年（公元752年）的《外台秘要》卷二十一收录了天竺医师的眼科治疗方法和验方，其中提到齐州的谢道人从天竺僧人处学习眼科医术，认为人体是由地、火、水、风四元素构成。鉴真和尚也曾请一位外国眼科医生为自己治疗眼病。

northern shore of the Mediterranean Sea, from Greece to Yugoslavia, Italy, Provence in southern France, and Spain. The second is along the Danube River Basin, extending from Southeast Europe, Central Europe, the Netherlands and Belgium. The westward spreading of millet created a precedent for European primitive agriculture.

Millet was introduced to East Asia in such countries as Korea and Japan via the Shandong peninsula or the Liaodong peninsula. In Japan, millet was cultivated at the end of the Jomon Period (14500 B.C. −5000 B.C.). The role it played in agriculture became less important after rice was introduced. In short, from the Prehistoric Period to the Medieval Period, millet was already cultivated in most of the known areas of the world at that time.

The strong stress resistance of millet and low price make it possible to obtain a certain amount of production in relatively barren lands for relief in bad years. Its edible value was indispensable in the ancient and the Medieval Period of the world. The Roman Empire took millet as an important crop throughout the agrarian society. Millet played an important role in promoting its socio-economic development and cultural prosperity.

Henan is one of the places of origin of the soybean. Soybean has been an extremely valuable agricultural resource of the Henan people from ancient times to the present, and it is also a kind of crop which produces nutrient-rich cooking oil and feed. Compared with millet, the time when soybean spread from Henan to the world is relatively late. Henan soybean was introduced to Japan prior to 3,000 B.C. 2,000 years later since then, it was introduced to North Korea. Before the Han Dynasty, soybean was not known in southern China. Therefore, the cultivation of soybean was promoted between the 1st century and 15th century in southern Asia. It was introduced to countries in Southeast Asia such as Indonesia in the 13th century. From the year 1740 to 1879, soybean was introduced to America, Africa and Oceania from Europe.

Ⅳ. The Exchange of Medical Technology, Pharmacy, Astronomy and Calendars

1. The Exchange of Medical Technology

The opening of the Silk Road facilitated not only the exchange of commodities between the East and the West, but also the exchange of medical technology. Long

研究中国科学技术史的权威英国学者李约瑟先生认为，这一时期西方医学主要带给中国两件事物："穿颅术"和"底也伽"。前者是一种外科手术，而后者是一种药物。人们普遍相信，东罗马医生在中国至尊的皇帝身上实践过穿颅手术，并且把药物底也伽送给他服用。

眼部疾病长期困扰着唐高宗李治（图2-4），由于久治不愈，他不得不委托皇后武则天代替自己批阅奏折。这一举措让女政治家武则天掌握权力，并逐渐确立起权威。李治去世以后，武则天进一步独揽大权，甚至废

图2-4 唐高宗像

Fig. 2-4 A portrait of Emperor Gaozong of the Tang Dynasty

黜自己的儿子，自立为中国历史上唯一的女皇。

为了给皇帝治病，罗马医生被召进宫廷。公元683年，李治病重，头部眩晕、眼睛失明，召侍医秦鸣鹤诊治。秦鸣鹤认为，用针刺穿皇帝的头部给皇帝放血，可以治愈。皇后武则天闻言，非常愤怒，叱责秦鸣鹤："该杀！竟敢刺皇帝的脑袋？"李治却说："我正苦于头重，刺出血来未必不是好事。"经过手术，李治的病情得到了缓解。

before the Tang Dynasty, Indian medicine had exerted an important influence on Chinese medicine. Many Indian medical works, especially Buddhist medical books, had been translated into Chinese. By the time of the Tang Dynasty, the influence of Indian medical works was further strengthened, and Indian ophthalmology with special efficacy was an important field in which India had an impact on the Tang Dynasty. The twenty-first volume of Wang Tao's *Medical Secrets of an Official* which was finished in 752 A.D., in the period of Emperor Xuanzong of the Tang Dynasty, collected the ophthalmologic treatment methods and prescriptions of Indian physicians. It mentioned that Taoist Xie from Qizhou learned ophthalmologic medicine from Indian monks and believed that the human body was composed of four elements: earth, fire, water and wind. Monk Jianzhen once asked a foreign ophthalmologist to treat his own eye disease. According to a British scholar, Joseph Needham, the authority on the study of Chinese history of science and technology, western medicine during this period mainly brought two things to China: craniotomy and theriac (one medical compound). The former was a surgical operation while the latter was a drug. It was widely believed that the doctor from Eastern Rome performed a craniotomy on the Chinese supreme emperor and gave him the drug.

Eye diseases had long plagued Li Zhi, Emperor Gaozong of the Tang Dynasty (fig.2—4). Because of his long-term affliction, he had to entrust his Empress Wu Zetian to read and comment on the memorials for him. This move enabled the female statesman Wu Zetian to master power and gradually establish authority. After Li Zhi's death, Wu Zetian further assumed arbitrary power, and she even dethroned her sons to become the only empress in Chinese history.

A Roman doctor was summoned to the imperial palace to treat the Emperor. In 683 A.D., Li Zhi was seriously ill with a dizzy head and blind eyes, so he called in Qin Minghe, the imperial physician. Qin Minghe thought that it was possible to cure the Emperor by puncturing the emperor's head with a needle and bloodletting. On hearing this, Empress Wu Zetian was very angry and rebuked Qin Minghe, "You should be killed! How dare you puncture the Emperor in the head?" Li Zhi, however, said, "I'm suffering from a heavy head, and puncturing may not be a bad thing." After the surgery, Li Zhi's suffering was relieved.

Westerners who came to China during the Medieval Period often took their

中古时期来华的西方人士，往往以自己国家作为姓氏。秦鸣鹤来自大秦，一般认为他是一位入华的景教徒。当时无论是来自印度的佛教僧人，还是来自叙利亚的景教教士，都喜欢以行医配合传教，取得朝野的尊重。

唐代文献普遍记载，印度和东罗马医生都擅长治疗眼疾。其中，印度眼科医生懂得用金针剔除白内障，而罗马医生更让中国人感到惊讶，他们掌握了穿颅术的技巧。这种希腊名医希波克拉底曾经记载过的开颅技术，被景教徒翻译成波斯文和阿拉伯文，流传到西亚和中亚地区，又通过不同途径传播到中国，被中国人惊为神技。不过，创伤较大、血肉淋漓的手术毕竟不容易被一般人接受，说到西方医学对中国的影响，药物的传播可能更为重要。

2.药学交流

从隋唐时期开始，香料和药材已经成为中国从海外进口的大宗产品，此后历朝历代一直在进口贸易中占有重要地位。公元667年，也就是李治因为久病不愈，任命太子监国的那一年，拜占庭使者献给他一种"神奇的药物"——底也伽。这是一种著名的药物，创自古罗马，由阿拉伯医生带到中国，其中最主要的成分是鸦片。

鸦片罂粟种原产于莱茵河流域，最迟在公元前14世纪时，已经传遍包括西亚在内的环地中海沿岸地区。塞浦路斯人首先发明了鸦片采集技术，而埃及人发现了鸦片的药用价值，这些知识随后又传回欧洲。从古希腊时代起，欧洲人就将鸦片作为药品来使用。

唐宋元三朝，中医逐渐发现鸦片切实有效的药用功能，同时罂粟因为美丽的花型，逐渐被驯化成一种观赏植物。然而，从明中期开始，鸦片逐渐变成帝国主义者牟取暴利的工具。

由于有大量外来药材被引进黄河流域，随之出现了记载外来药材的

country as their surname. Qin Minghe came from Da Qin, and he was generally believed to be a Nestorian from Syria. At that time, both Buddhist monks from India and Nestorian priests from Syria tended to preach with medical practice to gain respect from the imperial court and the common people.

Most of the literature of the Tang Dynasty recorded that doctors from India and East Rome all excelled in treating eye diseases. Indian ophthalmologists knew how to remove cataracts with gold needles, while Roman doctors amazed the Chinese more by their mastering of the technique of craniotomy. This kind of technique, which was recorded by the famous Greek doctor Hippocrates, was translated into Persian and Arabic by the Nestorians, spreading to West and Central Asia, and then to China through different channels. Despite the miraculous skills, surgery was more traumatic and bloodier, so it was not generally accepted by common people. The spread of drugs might play a more important role when it came to western medicine's impact on China.

2. The Exchange of Pharmacy

From the Sui and Tang Dynasties, spices and medicinal materials became China's bulk products imported from overseas. Thereafter they occupied an important position in the import trade in all dynasties. In 667 A.D., the year when Li Zhi appointed the prince to supervise the country because of his long illness, Byzantine envoys offered the Emperor a "magic drug", theriac. It was a famous drug that originated in ancient Rome and was brought to China by Arabic doctors, of which the most important ingredient was opium.

Native to the Rhine Valley, by the 14th century B.C., opium poppies had spread throughout the Mediterranean Rim, including West Asia. The Cypriots first developed the technology of collecting opium, and the Egyptians discovered the medicinal value of opium, which was then passed back to Europe. During ancient Greek times, Europeans began to use opium as medicine.

During the Tang, Song and Yuan Dynasties, the effective medicinal function of opium was gradually discovered in Chinese medicine, and at the same time, the poppy was gradually domesticated into an ornamental plant because of its beautiful flower. However, since the middle of the Ming Dynasty, opium gradually became a tool for the imperialists to make huge profits.

Since a large quantity of exotic medicinal materials were introduced into the

专著，其中就有河南荥阳人郑虔的《胡本草》七卷。

3. 天文历法交流

外来天文学对唐朝产生了重要的影响，主要表现在印度和波斯天文学的传入。这和入唐的外国人，如印度人、波斯人有着密切的联系。古代印度的天文学历史悠久，对周边国家影响甚大。《旧唐书》就记载其国"有文字，善天文算历之术"。虽然印度天文学很早就进入中国，然而其高潮却出现在唐代。唐初所修撰的《隋书》中的《经籍志》就记载了当时流传的天竺天文学方面的书籍。

来自天竺的瞿昙家族在唐朝世代从事天文历算职业，对唐代天文历法的影响非常大。瞿昙罗在武则天时期造《光宅历》，他在高宗和武后时期长期在洛阳担任太史令，主持修撰历法。瞿昙罗的儿子瞿昙悉达在天文学方面成就更为突出。他在玄宗开元年间担任太史监，开元六年（公元718年），瞿昙悉达受玄宗诏翻译了天竺《九执历》，引入了许多新的天文学知识和概念。瞿昙悉达还编撰了《开元占经》，该书集唐以前星占学说之大成，是研究中国古代天文学和星占学的重要资料。瞿昙悉达的儿子和孙子后来也都从事天文工作。瞿昙家族四代为唐朝政府从事天文工作，为唐朝天文学的进一步发展做出了重要的贡献。

除了瞿昙家族之外，在唐朝天文机构任职的印度人还有迦叶孝威和僧人俱摩罗。《旧唐书》就记载了迦叶孝威"天竺法"推算日月食的方法。《旧唐书》还记载了天竺僧人俱摩罗所传断日食法。可见当时源自天竺的数家历法都被唐朝天文机构所知晓，只是瞿昙氏的历法使用比较普遍，与唐朝制定的历法参考使用。

除天文学之外，印度算法也被介绍到唐朝。

唐代传入黄河流域的外来历法还有《七曜历》。《七曜历》广泛流行于波斯、天竺及粟特人中。据唐代书籍记载，当时此历法已经传入了唐朝，

Yellow River Basin, there appeared some monographs on the foreign medicinal materials, including the 7 volumes of *Hu Herbal Medicine* by Zheng Qian from Xingyang County, Henan Province.

3. The Exchange of Astronomy and Calendars

Foreign astronomy had an important influence on the Tang Dynasty, which was mainly manifested through the introduction of Indian and Persian astronomy. This was closely related to foreigners who came to China during the Tang Dynasty, such as Indians and Persians. Astronomy in ancient India had a long history and had a great influence on neighboring countries. *Old Book of Tang* recorded that India had a writing system and a good astronomical calendar. Although Indian astronomy was introduced to China very early, it reached its climax during the Tang Dynasty. *Confucian Classics Records* in *The Book of the Sui Dynasty* compiled during the early Tang Dynasty collected the books on Indian astronomy, which were widespread at that time.

The Gautama family from India engaged in astronomy careers during the Tang Dynasty, and had a great influence on the astronomical calendar of the Tang Dynasty. Gautama made the *Guangzhai Calendar* during the period of Empress Wu Zetian. In the period of Emperor Gaozong and Empress Wu Zetian, Gautama served as the imperial astronomer in Luoyang, and presided over the revision of the calendar. Gautama Siddha, the son of Gautama, made more outstanding achievements in astronomy during the Tang Dynasty. During the Kaiyuan Period of Emperor Xuanzong, Gautama Siddha served as a court historian. In the sixth year of the Kaiyuan Period (718 A.D.), Gautama Siddha was instructed by Emperor Xuanzong to translate the Indian *Navagraha Calendar*, introducing extensive new astronomical knowledge and concepts. Gautama Siddha also compiled the *Treatise on Astrology of the Kaiyuan Era*, a comprehensive collection of astrological works before the Tang Dynasty, which was important material for the study of ancient astronomy and astrology in China. Gautama Siddha's sons and grandsons also undertook astronomical work. Four generations of the Gautama family engaged in astronomical work for the Tang government, and they made important contributions to the further development of astronomy throughout the Tang Dynasty.

In addition to the Gautama family, the Indians who served in the Tang Dynasty astronomical institutions included Kasyapa and the Buddhist monk Kumara. *Old*

唐人对此也有所了解。

除了天竺和波斯之外,其他一些国家也经常进献各种天文书籍以及通晓天文的学者。

Book of Tang recorded the Indian method of calculating the eclipse of the sun and the moon by Kasyapa. *Old Book of Tang* also recorded the method of calculating the solar eclipse handed down by the Buddhist monk Kumara. It could be seen that several calendars originating from India were known by the astronomical institutions of the Tang Dynasty. Gautama's calendar was commonly used, along with the calendar formulated during the Tang Dynasty as a reference.

In addition to astronomy, the Indian mathematics was also introduced to the Tang Dynasty.

Foreign calendars that were introduced to the Yellow River Basin during the Tang Dynasty also included the *Seven Luminaries Calendar*. The *Seven Luminaries Calendar* was widely used among Persians, Indians and Sogdians. It could be found in some books of the Tang Dynasty that the calendar had been introduced to the Tang Dynasty and people of the Tang Dynasty gained some understanding of this calendar.

In addition to India and Persia, other countries also regularly contributed some astronomical books and scholars to China.

第三章

思想交流与文化传播

Chapter III

Ideological Exchange and Cultural Communication

丝绸之路带来古代社会规模罕见的人口流动，不同族群与文化循着这条通道，在地中海到河南之间的广大范围内迁移和扩散。在这个过程中，中国文化从欧亚各个民族和地区的文化中吸取了丰富的营养，从而茁壮成长。

一、宗教的传入与演化

丝绸之路促进了中外文化交流，最高级的形态之一便是宗教交流。商贸的往来带动了人口的流动，进而促使多种宗教循着丝路向中国传播。其中影响最深远的是佛教。

佛教沿着丝绸之路传入中国，从而深刻地影响了中国的文化生态。

佛教最初传入中国约在西汉末年，两汉之际来自大月氏等国的僧侣，已经通过口耳相传，把一些关于佛教的教义和信息散播到中原地区。东汉时期，丝绸之路在班超等人的努力下再次开通，佛教乘此时机正式传入中国。最早的一部汉译佛经《四十二章经》在其序言里讲述了一个"白马驮经"的传奇故事。

据云，汉明帝夜里梦见一位遍身金色的神人，头顶发光，飞翔在宫殿前。梦境让汉明帝兴奋莫名，次日询问群臣，博学的大臣傅毅回答："西方有神，称为佛，就像您梦到的那样。"于是汉明帝派出使者，到大月氏求取佛经。摄摩腾、竺法兰两位高僧跟随使团来到中国。

这个使团给中国带回佛经、佛造像，以及跪拜仪轨。汉明帝命人将佛像绘制在宫室和陵墓上，他是中国第一个信仰佛教的皇帝。本来作为一种刚刚传入的外来宗教，中土佛教信徒主要是来华经商的中亚人士。但佛教传来之际，恰逢难得的良机：中国思想界开始对超自然的力量产生兴趣，而上流社会则狂热地追求着成仙和长生不老的美梦。佛教满足了当时中国精英阶层的精神需要，因此很快从洛阳推广到中国各地，而洛阳也成了中古时期中国佛教的信仰中心。皇室和上层社会对宗教活动的热衷让洛阳的

The Silk Road brought about extraordinary population movements in ancient times. Different ethnic groups and cultures followed this passage to migrate and spread throughout the vast area between the Mediterranean and Henan. During this course, Chinese culture absorbed rich nutrition from the culture of Eurasian nationalities and regions, and thus thrived.

I. Introduction and Evolution of Religions

The Silk Road promoted communication between Chinese and foreign cultures, of which the most advanced form was religious exchanges. Commerce and trade along the Silk Road led to the flow of the population, which in turn promoted the introduction of many religions to China along the Silk Road. The most far-reaching influential religion was Buddhism.

Buddhism was introduced into China through the Silk Road, thus profoundly influencing the cultural ecology of China.

Buddhism first came to China around the end of the Western Han Dynasty. During the Western and Eastern Han Dynasties, monks from Darouzhi and other countries had spread some Buddhist doctrines to the Central Plains by word of mouth. During the Eastern Han Dynasty, the Silk Road was reopened with the efforts of Ban Chao and others, which facilitated the official introduction of Buddhism into China. The earliest Chinese translation of the Buddhist scriptures, *The Sutra in Forty-two Sections*, tells a legendary story of "a white horse carrying the sutra" in the preface.

It was said that Emperor Ming of the Eastern Han Dynasty dreamed of a shining golden saint flying in front of the palace during the night. This dream excited Emperor Ming and he summoned his ministers for an explanation the next day. Fu Yi, a learned minister replied, "As Your Majesty dreamed of, there was a western god named Buddha." The Emperor then sent a delegation to Darouzhi to seek Buddhist scriptures. And two senior monks, Kasyapamatanga (She Moteng) and Dharmaranya (Zhu Falan) came to China along with the delegation.

This delegation brought Buddhist scriptures, Buddha statues, and rituals back to China. The Emperor Ming of the Han Dynasty ordered that the Buddha be painted in the palaces and mausoleums, and he became the first emperor in China

佛教发展非常迅速。据《洛阳伽蓝记》记载，北魏时仅洛阳一座城市就拥有大小寺庙1 367所。

洛阳白马寺是中土寺院年代最早的一座。古寺坐落在邙山南麓洛河北岸，相传这里是东汉明帝永平年间（58—75）接待摄摩腾、竺法兰两位僧人的馆舍，后成为中国第一座官方营建的佛教寺院。寺中的清凉台即摄摩腾和竺法兰翻译佛经之处。二人圆寂后也安葬于白马寺中。直到晚清时期白马寺尚有汉魏遗物保存。比如，清代状元毕沅（1730—1797）在其《中州金石记》中著录，清代白马寺大殿左侧苑中，尚保存着一座北魏时期的白马寺造像幢，造像幢上雕刻有佛像50余尊，十分精美。清末到民国初年，白马寺的伽蓝殿内还发现过一尊造型秀美的汉白玉弥勒菩萨造像，风格为北魏或东魏之作，造像身高2.16米，为当时同类造像中体积相当硕大者。该造像今藏于美国波士顿美术博物馆。遗憾的是，因为多次遭到战乱破坏，现在白马寺内最古老的建筑是建于金大定十五年（公元1175年）的齐云塔（图3-1），比建寺的年代晚了一千多年。该塔也是洛阳现存最古老的地面建筑。

作为中国佛教祖庭，白马寺长期是中国译经活动的中心。来自西域各国的高僧历尽跋涉之苦，携来大量经卷，他们聚集在白马寺，组成规模庞大的译经道场，所以古人有"经来白马寺"的名言，民间也有"白马驮经"的传说。

"白马驮经"的故事，魏晋时期已有流传。相传摄摩腾、竺法兰两位最早来华的高僧用一匹白马驮着经书来到洛阳。这种传说显然受到了洛阳本地古老的"龙马负图"故事的影响。其实白马寺为中国早期寺庙常见的名字，并不限于洛阳一地。也有旧说认为，白马寺得名于一个西域的宗教故事："相传云外国国王尝毁破诸寺，唯招提寺未及毁坏。夜有一白马绕塔悲鸣，即以启王，王即停坏诸寺。因改'招提'以为'白马'。故诸寺立名多取则焉。"现代学者则认为，"白马"很可能是梵语词"padma"的音译，即"赤莲花"之意。莲花在佛教中极受推崇，"padma"经常见于

who worshiped Buddhism. When Buddhism was newly introduced to the Central Plains, the believers were mainly merchants from Central Asia. But meanwhile there came this opportunity: the Chinese intellectual community began to take an interest in the supernatural, and the upper classes were enthusiastically pursuing immortality. Buddhism satisfied the spiritual needs of the Chinese elites at that time, so it quickly spread from Luoyang to all parts of China. As a result, Luoyang became the center of Chinese Buddhism during the Medieval Period. The enthusiasm of the royal family and the upper classes for religious activities contributed to the rapid development of Buddhism in Luoyang. According to *Temples and Monasteries in Luoyang*, during the Northern Wei Dynasty, there were 1,367 temples in Luoyang alone.

The White Horse Temple in Luoyang was the first among the Central-Plains Buddhist temples. Situated on the north bank of the Luohe River and the south side of Mountain Mang, the ancient temple was said to have been built during the Yongping Period of Emperor Ming of the Eastern Han Dynasty (58A.D.–75A.D.). It was the first Buddhist temple sponsored by the royal court in China. The Refreshing Terrace in the temple served as a translation workshop where Kasyapa-matanga (She Moteng) and Dharmaranya (Zhu Falan) translated Buddhist scriptures into Chinese. The two monks were buried in the White Horse Temple after they passed away. Until the late Qing Dynasty, there were still Han and Wei remains preserved in White Horse temple. For example, Bi Yuan (1730 A.D.–1797 A.D.), the champion scholar (the first place winner in the imperial examination) during the Qing Dynasty, in his *History of Bronze and Stone Inscriptions in Henan*, recorded that in the left section of White Horse Temple during the Qing Dynasty, there remained an artwork of the Northern Wei Dynasty where more than 50 statues of beautiful Buddha were carved. A grand white marble Maitreya statue of the Wei Dynasty style was found in the White Horse Temple sometime between the late Qing Dynasty to the early Republic of China. The statue was 2.16 meters tall, a very large statue for its type at that time, and it is now housed in the Museum of Fine Arts Boston. Regrettably, because of many wars and destruction, the oldest building in the White Horse Temple is the Qiyun Pagoda (fig. 3–1). It was built in the fifteenth year of the Dading Period of the Jin Dynasty (1175 A.D.), which was over a thousand years later than the establishment of the temple. This pagoda is also the oldest surviving above-ground building in Luoyang at present.

佛经,一般翻译为"钵头摩"或"波头摩"。

　　洛阳白马寺的译经事业盛极一时。在众多译者中,东汉末年来华的安世高是最为杰出的一位。据僧传记载,安世高名清,字世高,原是安息国太子。他自幼聪颖好学、博识多才,医学、天文无所不精,甚至还通晓鸟兽的语言。安世高佛法精深,教化广披西域各地,他怀着崇高的

图3-1　齐云塔　摄影:周畅
Fig. 3-1 The Qiyun Pagoda

As the birthplace of Chinese Buddhism, the White Horse Temple has long been recognized as the center of Chinese sutra translation. Eminent monks from the countries of the Western Regions brought to China large numbers of scriptures despite all kinds of hardships. They gathered in the White Horse Temple and established a large-scale translation institution. Therefore, there was a famous old saying "Buddhist scriptures all came to the White Horse Temple" and the folk legend of "a white horse carrying the sutra".

The story of "a white horse carrying the sutra" was circulated throughout the Wei and Jin Dynasties. According to the legend, the first two monks who came to China, Kasyapamatanga and Dharmaranya, traveled to Luoyang with a white horse carrying the sutra. This kind of legend was obviously influenced by the ancient Luoyang local story of "Dragon-horse emerged from the Yellow River carrying a chart on his back" (the story is about how Fu Xi, the first mythical emperor of China, made the Bagua based on the chart on the back of a dragon-house as it rose from the Yellow River). White Horse Temple was also allegedly a common name of ancient Chinese temples, not limited to the one in Luoyang. There was also an old saying where White Horse Temple got its name from a religious story from Western Regions: some king once tried to destroy all the temples except the one named "Zhaoti", where one night a white horse neighed sorrowfully around a tower. The king was deeply touched and stopped destroying the temples. After that the name of this temple was changed from Zhaoti to the White Horse Temple, and from then on, many temples were called White Horse temple. However, modern scholars believe that "bai ma" (white horse) is probably the transliteration of the Sanskrit word "padma", which means "red lotus". Lotuses are highly respected in Buddhism, and "padma" is often found in Buddhist scriptures, generally translated as "botoumo".

Buddhist scripture translation in the White Horse Temple was once a thriving and important undertaking. Among many translators, An Shigao was the most outstanding, who came to China at the end of the Eastern Han Dynasty. According to his biography, An Shigao was originally the Prince of Parthia (ancient Iran); his given name was Qing and his courtesy name was Shigao. He was intelligent and knowledgeable, and he had an excellent mastery of medicine and astronomy. He was said to have a skill of understanding the language of birds and beasts. Being an expert of Buddhist study, whose teachings were widely known in Western Regions,

宗教热情来到中国，并且迅速地掌握汉语。安世高于汉桓帝建和元年（公元147年）来到洛阳，驻锡白马寺。当时佛教传入中国已有相当长的时间，在宫廷内和社会上都有一些信徒。但佛经的介绍多凭僧人口耳相传，难免与经意有相左之处。因此，安世高着手将佛经译为汉文。此后二十多年间，他先后翻译了佛教经典约34部，共40卷。安世高在中国传教约四十年，对中国佛教影响深远。现代佛学界将他译介的佛经称为"旧译"，将后秦高僧鸠摩罗什所译称为"新译"，两者相辅而行。

比安世高稍晚的另一个西域人佛图澄（232—348）沿着同样的道路来到洛阳传法。佛图澄的弟子道安（312—385）是第一位集大成的中国僧人。至此，佛教终于被中国文化成功地消化吸纳。

像安世高、佛图澄那样来华传教的西域僧人，为数众多。仅北魏宣武帝时，就有"时佛教盛于洛阳。沙门自西域来者，三千余人，魏主别为之立永宁寺千余间以居之"的记载。这座永宁寺，被《洛阳伽蓝记》记载于全书的首篇，因为它是汉魏洛阳城规模最宏大，也最富丽堂皇的寺院。

佛教的传入及兴盛促进了洛阳寺庙文化的繁荣。从白马寺算起，这里曾有1 300多座寺庙，佛教活动繁荣的盛况可见一斑。永宁寺在白马寺东南约1.5千米处，它的修建是为了分流白马寺无法容纳的庞大僧团，同时它也是北魏重修洛阳城时，唯一规划在宫城侧畔的皇家寺院，地位显赫。在中国佛教建筑史上，永宁寺及寺内的永宁寺塔有重要价值。北魏以后，中国的佛寺建筑逐渐形成了汉化的风格。遗憾的是，永宁寺最终毁于火灾，考古发现永宁寺遗址的土壤有明显的火焚痕迹，美轮美奂的建筑尽数付诸焦土。

北魏时期（386—534），佛教"依山为寺"盛行。河南省洛阳市洛龙区伊河畔坐落着著名的世界文化遗产——龙门石窟（图3-2）。这里是古代中国的佛教圣地，在大禹"凿龙门，辟伊阙"，制服了水患后，对中国人来说，"登龙门，望伊阙"，就意味着"观文、武、周、召遗化"，凭吊古代圣贤。自公元494年北魏迁都洛阳，龙门又成了高僧译经传法的

An Shigao came to China with lofty religious enthusiasm and quickly mastered the Chinese language. He came to Luoyang and settled in the White Horse Temple in the first year of the Jianhe Period of the Emperor Huan of the Han Dynasty (147 A.D.). At that time, Buddhism had been introduced to China for long, and there were believers both in the royal court and among the common people. However, Buddhist scriptures were often spread and popularized by word of mouth among monks, so there were inevitably some misunderstandings. Therefore, An Shigao began to translate the Buddhist scriptures into Chinese. In the following twenty years, he translated about thirty-four Buddhist scriptures, adding up to forty volumes. An Shigao preached Buddhism in China for about 40 years and had a profound influence on Chinese Buddhism. Modern Buddhist scholars refer to the Buddhist scriptures An Shigao translated as "old translations". The translations of Monk Kumarajiva in Later Qin are referred to as "new translations", and the two complement one another.

Later than An Shigao, Buddhacinga (232 A.D.−348 A.D.), from some small western country, came to Luoyang via the same road to spread Buddhism. Dao'an, a disciple of Buddhacinga (312 A.D.−385 A.D.), was the first Chinese monk to epitomize Buddhism, which was hitherto successfully assimilated by Chinese culture.

There were large numbers of monks from western regions like An Shigao and Buddhacinga who came to China to spread Buddhism. During the reign of Emperor Xuanwu of the Northern Wei Dynasty alone, it was recorded that "Buddhism flourished in Luoyang, and there were more than 3,000 monks from the west. The Emperor of the Wei Dynasty established the Yongning Temple to accommodate them." The Yongning Temple was the largest and the most magnificent one in Luoyang during the Han and Wei Dynasties. This temple was documented in the very first chapter of the famous historical classic *Temples and Monasteries in Luoyang*.

The introduction and prevalence of Buddhism led to a phenomenal temple culture in Luoyang. Besides the White Horse Temple, there were once 1,300 temples established here, a phenomenon of booming Buddhist activities. The Yongning Temple, about 1.5 kilometers southeast of the White Horse Temple, was built as another monastery to accommodate the huge Buddhist sangha when the White Horse Temple was overcrowded. At the same time, it was the only regal-sponsored temple situated closely next to the Palace City when the City of Luoyang was rebuilt

图3-2 龙门石窟全景　摄影：周畅
Fig. 3-2 Panorama of Longmen Grottoes

中心。在伊河两岸的群山上，曾有多座寺庙依山而建，留下了美轮美奂的石窟。依石窟造像而存的造像记录多为书法艺术精品，其中最有名的就是《龙门二十品》（图3-3）。北魏太和十九年（公元495年），孝文帝为印度高僧跋陀建造了少林寺。另一位印度高僧菩提达摩在寺中面壁十年，传下禅宗心印。禅宗是中国本土化的佛教派别，它把佛教哲学发展到新的高度。现在，中国禅宗在海内外吸引了一大批信仰者，它是佛教最有活力的一个流派。

盛大的译经活动是中国文化史上的盛事。隋唐时期佛经翻译往往是在皇室支持下进行的。隋炀帝登基后，在洛阳的宫廷里设内道场作为宫廷佛教研究院，隋大业二年（公元606年），炀帝还在洛阳洛河之滨的上林园设翻经馆，由僧彦琮主其事，组织中外僧人译经。唐高宗、武则天时期的洛阳也有大量来自中亚和印度的僧侣。天竺僧菩提流志、宝思惟、慧智，于阗僧实叉难陀，都在洛阳译经。南天竺高僧菩提流志于唐永淳二年（公元683年）来华之后在洛阳福先寺译经11部，后又在长安译经，开元十一年（公元723年）住洛阳长寿寺，开元十五年（公元727年）葬于龙门。北天竺僧人宝思惟于唐长寿二年（公元693年）来到洛阳，先后在天宫寺、佛授记寺、福先寺译经，后在龙门创天竺寺并圆寂于此。

during the Northern Wei Dynasty. The Yongning Temple and the Yongning Temple Pagoda were of great value in the history of Chinese Buddhist architecture. After the Northern Wei Dynasty, the Chinese Buddhist temple architecture gradually developed a Chinese style. Regrettably, the Yongning Temple was eventually destroyed by fire. Archaeological findings found signs of burnt remains where the Yongning Temple purportedly used to stand.

During the Northern Wei Dynasty (386 A.D.–534 A.D.), Buddhism was at the peak stage of "building temples on or by the mountain". Longmen Grottoes (fig. 3–2), a world-famous cultural heritage site, is located on the banks of the Yihe River in Luolong District, Luoyang, Henan. This used to be a holy place of Buddhism in ancient China. After Yu the Great (one of the greatest mythical ancestors of Chinese civilization) "dug Longmen, built Yique (Gate of the Yihe River)" and tamed the floods, for Chinese people, the saying "climbing the Longmen mountain and overlooking Yique" came to mean recollecting ancient cultural legacies and paying tribute to the ancient sages. Since the capital was relocated to Luoyang during the Northern Wei Dynasty in 494 A.D., Longmen had become the center of Buddhism scriptures translation. On the mountains that overlook Yihe River, a great many temples were built, leaving behind beautiful grottoes. Most of the building records of the statues preserved in the caves were calligraphy art works, of which the most famous is *The Twenty Select Pieces of Calligraphy of Longmen* (fig. 3–3). In the 19th year of the Taihe Period of the Northern Wei Dynasty (495 A.D.), Emperor Xiaowen built the Shaolin Temple for the Indian monk Bhadra. Another Indian monk, Bodhidharma practiced "wall-gazing" meditation in this temple for ten years and passed down Zen Buddhism, a localized Buddhism school in China that elevated Buddhist philosophy to a new level. Nowadays, as one of the most dynamic schools of Buddhism, Chinese Zen has attracted large numbers of enthusiasts around the world.

The translation of Buddhist scriptures was a significant event in the history of Chinese culture. During the Sui and Tang Dynasties, Buddhist scripture translations were carried out under the support of the royal court. After ascending the throne, Emperor Yang of the Sui Dynasty set up an internal research institute of Buddhism in the royal court. In the year 606 A.D., Emperor Yang established a sutra translation institute in Shanglin Garden by the side of Luohe River. In this institute, Buddhist

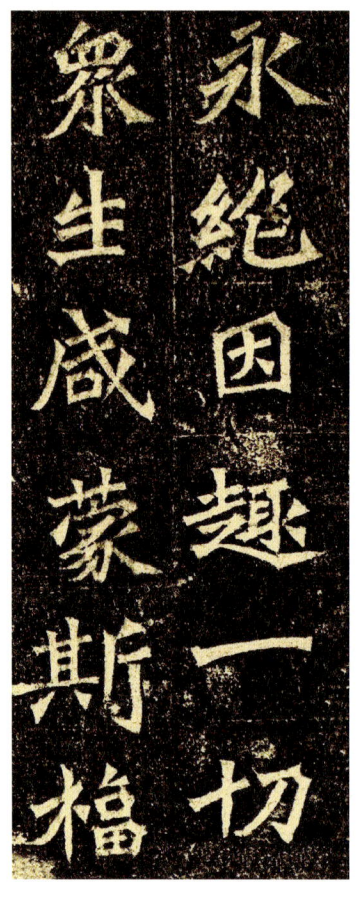

图3-3 龙门二十品（部分）
Fig. 3-3 Part of The Twenty Select Pieces of Calligraphy of Longmen

  这些译经活动中，最重要的一例是于阗高僧实叉难陀在武则天时期携梵本《华严经》来到洛阳。证圣元年（公元695年），实叉难陀受命在大遍空寺翻译此经。实叉难陀病故后，法藏等僧侣在佛授记寺继续该经的翻译。武则天多次到译场视察，施供食馔，还为译本撰写了序言。四年后，该经翻译完成，武则天在宫中听法藏宣讲经义，对于《华严经》深奥复杂的义理茫然不解，法藏就以殿前的金属狮子做比喻，撰写《金狮子章》来阐明。在武则天的支持下，法藏在洛阳创立了中国佛教的重要支派华严宗。

monk Yan Cong supervised and coordinated the work of Buddhist scripture translation. During the reign of Emperor Gaozong of the Tang Dynasty and Empress Wu Zetian, there were also large numbers of monks from Central Asia and India in Luoyang, including Indian monks such as Bodhiruci, Bao Siwei, Hui Zhi, Siksananda etc. After coming to China in the second year of Yongchun Period (683 A.D.), Bodhiruci, a Southern Indian monk, translated 11 sutras at the Fuxian Temple in Luoyang, and later continued his work in Chang'an. He lived in the Changshou Temple in Luoyang in the eleventh year of the Kaiyuan period (723 A.D.) and was buried in Longmen in the fifteenth year of the Kaiyuan period (727 A.D.). Bao Siwei, a Northern Indian monk, came to Luoyang in the second year of the Changshou period (693 A.D.) to translate scriptures at the Tiangong Temple, the Foshouji Temple, the Fuxian Temple and finally at the Tianzhu Temple in Longmen till he passed away there.

Among these translation activities, one of the most significant moments was the arrival of Siksananda, a senior monk from Khotan, who brought the *Avatamsaka Sutra* in Sanskrit language to Luoyang during the reign of Empress Wu Zetian. In the first year of Zhengsheng (695 A.D.), Siksananda was entrusted with the translation of this sutra in the Dabiankong Temple. After Siksananda, Fazang took over his unfinished work in the Foshouji temple. Wu Zetian visited the translation hall many times, offered dishes of food, and wrote a preface for the translated scriptures. Four years later, the translation was completed. Wu Zetian listened to Fazang teaching the sutra, which however she found too profound to understand. Fazang illustrated his teachings with the metal lions in front of the palace and he wrote the *Treatise on the Gold Lion* to clarify. With the support of Empress Wu Zetian, Fazang established an important school of Chinese Buddhism, the Huayan Sect.

Chinese Buddhism is divided into two sects: Exotoric and Esoteric Buddhism. Today's esoteric monks mainly originated from Tibetan Buddhism. But before the An Lushan Rebellion during the Tang Dynasty, Esoteric Buddhism used to play a dominant role in Buddhism prevailing in the Han nationality regions. During the Kaiyuan Period (713A.D.–741A.D.), Indian Buddhist monks Vajrabodhi, Subhakarasimha and Amoghavajra translated and spread Buddhist scriptures in Luoyang. They were known as the "Three Grand Masters of Kaiyuan". In the twelfth

中国佛教分显、密两宗,今天的密宗僧人主要来自藏传佛教。但在唐代安史之乱前,密宗在汉地佛教中也曾占有优势地位。开元年间(713—741)来到唐朝的天竺密宗高僧金刚智、善无畏和不空都曾在洛阳译经并传播密宗,他们号称"开元三大士"。善无畏在开元十二年(公元724年)随唐玄宗来到洛阳,并在大福先寺译出了密宗主要经典《大日经》,圆寂后就葬于龙门西山。金刚智到洛阳后曾用密宗的咒语祈雨,后圆寂于洛阳广福寺,葬于龙门。而金刚智的弟子不空也跟随师父来到洛阳从事译经活动。

除了中亚、南亚僧人来华传教,同一时期中国僧人也不乏西行求法的壮举。很多求法僧人都是从洛阳开始踏上旅程,比如,"魏宋云与惠生自洛阳西行四千里,至赤岭,乃出魏境,又西行,再期,至乾罗国而还。二月,达洛阳,得佛经一百七十部。"唐代求法僧人最著名的是玄奘(602—664)和义净(635—713)。玄奘是洛州缑氏(今河南洛阳偃师市缑氏镇)人。贞观十九年(公元645年)他从天竺回到长安,带回梵本经论657部。当时唐太宗驻跸洛阳宫,立即诏令他来洛阳相见。后玄奘从洛阳折回长安从事译经活动。显庆二年(公元657年)二月,唐高宗巡幸洛阳,玄奘随驾前来,在洛阳的积翠宫翻译佛教典籍。证圣元年(公元695年),义净游学天竺归国,带回经律梵本,武则天亲临洛阳上东门迎候,把他安排到佛授记寺译经。

佛教通过丝绸之路传入中国,丰富和活跃了中古时代中国的思想和文化。从永平求法,白马驮经,到禅宗立派,一花开五叶,中国思想在文化交流中走过了一个富于创造性的时代。

从丝绸之路传到中原的宗教,除了佛教以外,其他宗教在中国也有一定发展,对中国的思想文化产生了一定的影响。其中影响较大的有祆教、景教和摩尼教。

year of the Kaiyuan Period (724 A.D.), Subhakarasimha accompanied the Emperor Xuanzong to Luoyang, and translated the esoteric classic *Mahavairocana Tantra* at the Dafuxian Temple until he passed away and was buried in the Western Longmen Mountain. Vajrabodhi once performed prayers for rain in Luoyang with the Tantric mantra. He was buried in Longmen after he passed away in the Guangfu Temple. And Amoghavajra, Vajrabodhi's disciple, also went to Luoyang to engage himself in sutra translation.

Apart from the missionary undertakings on the part of the monks from Central Asia and South Asia, Chinese monks meanwhile also made significant efforts on their journeys to the west in the pursuit of scriptures of Dharma. Many of them departed from Luoyang. For instance, "Songyun and Hui Sheng of the Wei Dynasty made a four thousand li (Chinese mile) journey westward from Luoyang to Chiling, crossed the border and went on and finally arrived in Qianluo. In February they returned with 170 Buddhist sutras." Among these sutra seekers, the most famous monks were Xuanzang (602 A.D.–664 A.D.) and Yijing (635 A.D.–713 A.D.) in the Tang Dynasty. Xuanzang, a Luoyang native from Yanshi County, brought back 657 scriptures from India in the nineteenth year of the Zhenguan Period (645 A.D.). Emperor Taizong of the Tang Dynasty, who stayed in the Luoyang Palace at that time, immediately summoned Xuanzang to Luoyang to meet him. After Xuanzang returned to Chang'an, he engaged himself in translating the Buddhist scriptures. In February of the second year of the Xianqing Period (657 A.D.), Xuanzang accompanied the Emperor Gaozong of the Tang Dynasty to Luoyang and continued his translation career in the Jicui Palace of Luoyang. In the first year of Zhengsheng (695 A.D.), Yijing traveled to India to study Buddhism and brought back Buddhist scriptures. Empress Wu Zetian came to the Shangdong Gate of Luoyang to welcome Yijing back and made arrangements for him to translate Buddhist scriptures in the Foshouji Temple.

Via the Silk Road, Buddhism was introduced to China, which was a remarkable enrichment and inspiration for Chinese ideology and culture during the Medieval Period. From Emperor Ming of the Eastern Han Dynasty sending a delegation to seek Buddhist scriptures during the Yongping Period and a white horse carrying the sutra to the establishment of the Zen Buddhism, and the Zen Buddhism's development into five schools, this chapter of the history of Chinese ideology was a profoundly creative era of cultural exchange.

二、美术的东传与西渐

1. 丝绸之路上的河南美术

唐三彩是中国古代陶瓷文化的杰出代表，全称"唐代三彩低温铅釉陶器"，是在汉代低温铅釉彩陶器的基础上发展而来的，经过魏晋南北朝的发展，在唐代终于形成了璀璨的唐三彩文化，史称唐三彩。唐代以后，唐三彩艺术继续发展，形成了"宋三彩"、"辽三彩"、"明三彩"和"清三彩"。目前所发现的烧造唐三彩的窑址主要有三个，分别为巩义黄冶村窑址、铜川黄堡镇窑址和内丘邢窑窑址，目前普遍认为巩义窑是最早开始烧造唐三彩的。除上述三处烧造唐三彩的民窑窑址外，在河南荥阳、宝丰、鲁山、禹州、新密、济源、温县、武陟、登封等地均发现了唐三彩的烧造。其中巩义窑所生产的唐三彩，经洛阳通过隋唐大运河运送至扬州，然后由扬州通过海上丝绸之路传播至日本、朝鲜、西亚以及非洲地区，并导致了模仿中国唐三彩的"奈良三彩""新罗三彩""埃及三彩""波斯三彩"的出现。

日本与朝鲜是东亚地区唐三彩的主要发现地，其中日本留存、出土的唐三彩较多。日本铅釉陶大约产生于公元7世纪后半期，在奈良时代以前，日本生产的铅釉陶多为单彩的绿釉陶，并且主要是陶砖或陶棺等。进入奈良时代以后，逐渐出现了真正意义上的多彩铅釉陶。日本多彩铅釉陶的出现，除了与日本本土陶瓷业的发展有关，还有一个重要原因，那就是中国唐代三彩艺术的输出。目前，在日本约14个地点发现了唐三彩器物及其残片，主要集中在福冈、奈良和京都地区，多出土于宫殿、寺庙遗址以及墓葬中。从日本出土的唐三彩器物的纹饰、造型及釉彩技术来看，其明显受到了中国唐代三彩艺术的影响。日本学者认为在寺庙所发现的唐三彩可能是由日本遣唐使或僧人带回日本的。由于日本三彩器盛行于奈良

In addition to Buddhism that was introduced to the Chinese Central Plains via the Silk Road, other religions also spread to, developed in China and cast certain impacts on Chinese ideology and culture. Among them, the most influential ones were Zoroastrianism, Nestorianism and Manichaeism.

II. The Spread of Art from East to West

1. Fine Art of Henan on the Silk Road

Tang Sancai is an outstanding representative of ancient Chinese ceramic culture, with its full name "Tang Sancai low-temperature lead-glazed pottery". On the basis of the art of low-temperature lead-glazed pottery of the Han Dynasty, it was further developed in the Wei, Jin, the Northern and Southern Dynasties, and grew to be a brilliant Tang Sancai culture in the Tang Dynasty, historically known as the Tang Sancai. After the Tang Dynasty, the Sancai art continued to develop and there appeared "Song Sancai", "Liao Sancai", "Ming Sancai" and "Qing Sancai". At present, three main kiln sites have been found for firing Tang Sancai. They are the Huangye Village Kiln Site in Gongyi City, the Huangbao Township Kiln Site in Tongchuan City and the Xingyao Kiln Site in Neiqiu County. It is believed that the Gongyi Kiln is the earliest kiln site for firing Tang Sancai. In addition to the three above-mentioned folk kiln sites for firing Tang Sancai, other sites were found in Xingyang, Baofeng, Lushan, Yuzhou, Xinmi, Jiyuan, Wenxian, Wuzhi, Dengfeng and other places in Henan Province. The Tang Sancai produced by Gongyi kilns were transported to Yangzhou via the Sui-Tang Grand Canal in Luoyang, and then exported to Japan, Korea, West Asia and Africa via the Maritime Silk Road where people imitated the Chinese Tang Sancai and produced "Nara Sancai" "Xinluo Sancai" "Egyptian Sancai" and "Persian Sancai".

In East Asia, Tang Sancai was discovered mainly in Japan and Korea, especially in Japan where lead-glazed pottery was produced around the second half of the 7th century. Before the Nara era, most of the lead-glazed pottery produced in Japan was monochrome green-glazed pottery in the form of pottery bricks or coffins. After entering the Nara era, multi colored lead-glazed pottery, in its real sense, gradually appeared. In addition to the development of the local ceramic industry in Japan, the emergence of multi colored lead-glazed pottery had something to do with

时期，日本三彩又被称为"奈良三彩"。

朝鲜在20世纪二三十年代出土过一些唐代陶瓷，数量不多，其中庆州朝阳洞附近出土的一件完整的三彩三足鍑，其造型、彩斑与江苏扬州出土的唐三彩非常相似，与河南省巩义窑所出土的唐三彩也非常相似。

唐三彩在西亚地区的发现地与传播地主要是在伊拉克、伊朗。自1910年至1936年，法国、德国、伊朗的考古工作者先后在巴格达以北120公里处的萨马拉考古遗址进行考古发掘，出土了大量的中国陶器，其中有唐三彩形式的钵与盘，以及绿釉、黄釉瓷罐的碎片。根据日本陶瓷学者三上次男的研究，这些唐三彩是在中国唐代三彩艺术传入近东后由波斯仿制烧造的。

北非与东非也发现了唐三彩的踪影。非洲北部埃及开罗郊外的福斯塔特遗址出土了大量公元7世纪至公元16世纪的中国瓷片，大约有12 000多件，包含巩义窑唐三彩、邢州窑白瓷、越州窑瓷、龙泉窑青瓷、景德镇青白瓷、定窑系白瓷以及长沙窑瓷等。福斯塔特遗址出土的陶瓷一部分是由古代中国经由海上丝绸之路传入的，绝大部分是在中国陶瓷传入后由埃及当地仿制的。

2. 隋唐洛阳城对日本京都规划及建筑的影响

京都位于日本西部京都府南部，坐落在京都盆地的北半部和丹波高原的东部山区，是日本历史上著名的千年古都。公元794年，桓武天皇定都京都，开启了平安时代，京都又被称为平安京。平安京南北长约5.2公里，东西长约4.5公里，以朱雀大路为中心，城市分为右京和左京两个对称的部分，右京又称为"长安"，左京又称为"洛阳"，右京模仿长安城，左京模仿洛阳城。右京因地理原因，不久就被废弃了，只剩下左京洛阳城部分。平安京的选址参考了中国的风水思想，其城市规划主要效仿唐长安城，但左京洛阳城部分也借鉴了隋唐洛阳城的某些特点，如平安京中的铜驼、

the importation of the Tang Sancai art. At present, Tang Sancai objects and their fragments have been found in about 14 sites in Japan, mainly in Fukuoka, Nara and Kyoto, and they were mostly unearthed in palaces, temple sites, and tombs. Judging from the patterns, shapes, and the glaze techniques of the Tang Sancai objects unearthed in Japan, they were obviously influenced by the Chinese Sancai art of the Tang Dynasty. Japanese scholars believed that the Tang Sancai found in the temples may have been taken to Japan by Japanese envoys or monks. Because the Japanese Sancai art was prevalent in the Nara period, the Japanese Sancai was also called "Nara Sancai".

A small number of Tang Dynasty ceramics were unearthed in Korea in the 1920s and 1930s. Among them, a complete Sancai jar with three legs, was unearthed in Joyang-dong, Gyeongju. Its shape and color spots were highly similar to those unearthed in Yangzhou, Jiangsu Province and Gongyi Kiln, Henan Province.

In West Asia, Iraq and Iran are major places where Tang Sancai were discovered and spread. From 1910 to 1936, the archaeologists of France, Germany, and Iran successively carried out archaeological excavations at the Samara site, 120 kilometers north of Baghdad, and unearthed a large amount of Chinese pottery, including Tang Sancai jars and dishes, as well as fragments of green or yellow glazed porcelain jars. According to the Japanese scholar T. Mikami, these Sancai pieces were imitations of Tang Sancai by the Persians after Chinese Sancai art was introduced to the Near East.

Traces of Tang Sancai were also found in North and East Africa. About 12,000 Chinese porcelain fragments from the seventh to sixteenth centuries were unearthed at the Fustat Site on the outskirts of Cairo, Egypt, North Africa, including Gongyi kiln Tang Sancai, Xingzhou kiln white porcelain, Yuezhou kiln porcelain, Longquan kiln celadon, Jingdezhen celadon white porcelain, Dingyao kiln white porcelain and Changsha kiln porcelain. Some of the ceramics unearthed at the Fustat site were imported from ancient China via the Maritime Silk Road, and most of them were imitated locally in Egypt after the introduction of Chinese ceramics.

2. The Influence of Luoyang City in the Sui and Tang Dynasties on Kyoto City

Kyoto, located in the southern part of the Kyoto Prefecture in Western Japan, the northern half of the Kyoto Basin and the eastern mountainous area of the

教坊、丰财等坊名就模仿了隋唐洛阳城。日本人又称京都为"京洛"。"京洛"一词见于班固的《东都赋》："子徒习秦阿房之造天,而不知京洛之有制也。"班固笔下的"京洛"指东汉都城洛阳,而日本人所称的"京洛"可能是指平安京左京洛阳城。今天日本京都的一些地名、遗迹仍可以看出隋唐洛阳城的许多影子,如京都的东南西北中部分习惯上被称为"洛东""洛南""洛西""洛北"和"洛中",人们把出售的"丝织物"称为"京洛锦",把自制的抹茶饮料称为"洛水",学校直接命名洛阳工业学校和洛西中学校,亦有洛阳十三番朝会堂石刻的名称。唐长安城与洛阳城内建有大量的佛寺,日本平安京的规划设计也模仿了这一点,今天的日本京都仍有1 500多座佛寺,其中著名的有安国寺、大相国寺、唐招提寺、东大寺等。唐代长安、洛阳亦有安国寺、招提寺,宋代的开封则有著名的大相国寺,并且直到今天开封大相国寺、洛阳安国寺、洛阳偃师招提寺仍然存在。日本奈良、京都所遗存的大量佛寺建筑,无论是在建筑布局、建筑装饰,还是在建筑技术方面都受到了唐代两京建筑的影响。

3. 河南美术中的古希腊和古罗马文化因素

玻璃最早诞生于大约5 000年前的美索不达米亚平原,然后由美索不达米亚平原传播至埃及、希腊、罗马等地区,然后经由中亚地区传播至古代中国。1987年,洛阳东郊汉墓出土了一件非常完整的黄绿色长颈玻璃瓶,是典型的罗马搅胎吹制玻璃,自口沿至瓶底通体旋绕白色条纹,色调鲜明、造型优雅。除洛阳地区,广东、广西、山东、河北也都发现了类似的玻璃器物。20世纪初,加拿大人George Croft从一盗墓者手中收购了一件出土于河南古墓的玻璃瓶。与上述其他地区所发现的玻璃瓶相异的是,此玻璃瓶上有类似希腊战士的头像,这也更有力地说明了此玻璃瓶的古希腊风格来源。

20世纪中叶,洛阳中州路一战国墓葬出土若干"蜻蜓眼"料珠(图3-

Tamba Platea, is a well-known ancient capital of Japan for thousands of years. In 794, the Emperor Kammu made Kyoto the capital city, which opened the Heian Period. Kyoto was also known as Heian-kyō. Heian-kyō, about 5.2 kilometers long from north to south, 4.5 kilometers from east to west, was centered on Suzaku Road that divided the capital into two symmetrical parts: Ukyō and Sakyo ku. Ukyō was also called "Chang'an", and Sakyo ku "Luoyang". The former imitated Chang'an in architecture and the latter Luoyang. Because of certain geographical problems, Ukyō was soon abandoned, leaving only part of Sakyo ku. Heian-kyō was selected to be the capital city in reference to Chinese ideas about Fengshui (a system of laws considered to govern spatial arrangement and orientation in relation to the flow of energy, and whose favorable effects are taken into consideration in choosing the site of a building and designing), and its planning mainly followed the example of Chang'an City in the Tang Dynasty. However, the Luoyang Section in Sakyo ku also borrowed some features of Luoyang City during the Sui and Tang Dynasties. For example, the names of Tongtuo Fang (Fang refers to the residential area of the Tang Dynasty), Jiao Fang and Fengcai Fang in Heian-kyō are imitations of those of Luoyang City during the Sui and Tang Dynasties. The Japanese also called Kyoto "Jingluo". The word "Jingluo" can be found in Bangu's *Dongdu Fu* (*Lyrics on the East Capital*), "Sir, you only know that E'Pang Palace (the new imperial palace built by Emperor Qinshihuang) of Qin Dynasty soars into the clouds, thinking it a wonder without knowing the construction system of Jingluo." Here, Jingluo in Ban Gu's expression referred to Luoyang, the capital of the Eastern Han Dynasty, while Japan's "Jingluo" more likely referred to Sakyo ku of Heian-kyō. Today, the influence of Luoyang City in the Sui and Tang Dynasties can still be seen in some names of places and relics in Kyoto. For example, the east, south, west, north and the middle part of Kyoto are customarily called "Luodong" (East of Luoyang), "Luonan" (South of Luoyang), "Luoxi" (West of Luoyang), "Luobei" (North of Luoyang) and "Luozhong" (Luoyang Center), the silk fabric for sale is called "Jingluo brocade", homemade drinks with matcha are called "Luoshui", the schools were named as Luoyang Industrial School and Luoxi Middle School, and stone carving of the Luoyang Thirteenth Dynasties Hall. The planning and construction of Heian-kyō in Japan imitated the large number of Buddhist temples built in Chang'an and Luoyang in the Tang Dynasty. Today, there are still more than 1,500 Buddhist temples in Kyoto, including the famous Anguo

图3-4 洛阳中州路战国墓葬出土"蜻蜓眼"料珠

Fig. 3-4 Dragonfly eye glass beads unearthed from the tomb of the Warring States Period at Zhongzhou Road, Luoyang

4)。这种带有圈状套花工艺的玻璃样制品与公元前6世纪至公元前3世纪盛行于古埃及或腓尼基等地中海东岸国家的蜻蜓眼玻璃珠十分接近。无独有偶,河南固始侯古堆一号墓以及淅川徐家岭古墓也出土了一些蜻蜓眼钠钙玻璃珠,同类的料珠在中国山东、广东、湖北等地的战国古墓中亦有发现,似乎可以反映当时海上丝绸之路的开通。洛阳出土的西周晚期的青铜鼎上镶嵌有玻璃珠,足以说明当时西亚的玻璃制作技术已为中国所掌握。

车马出行图像是汉代绘画中常见的题材,初见于西汉晚期,盛行于东汉。目前所发现的车马出行图像以正侧面与四分之三侧面的为多,正面车马图像、正面骑马像、背面骑马像极其罕见。河南洛阳金村出土的一面战国晚期铜镜上(图3-5)铸有一正面骑马像,河南南阳新野出土的一块汉代画像砖绘有正面骑马像。除河南外,这种正面骑马图像也散见于山东的济宁、滕州等地区。上述背面骑或正面骑的图像不见于汉代之前的中国,但常见于古希腊地区以及希腊化时代的中亚地区。在古希腊、罗马艺术东传所途经的"欧亚草原丝绸之路"与"绿洲丝绸之路"上,都有这种正、

Temple, Daxiangguo Temple, Tang Zhaoti Temple and Dongda Temple. During the Tang Dynasty, there were also Anguo Temple and Zhaoti Temple in Chang'an and Luoyang, and in Song Dynasty, there was the famous Daxiangguo Temple in Kaifeng. Till now, the Daxiangguo Temple in Kaifeng, the Anguo Temple in Luoyang, and the Zhaoti Temple in Yanshi, Luoyang, are still in existence. A large number of the Buddhist temples that remain in Nara and Kyoto were influenced by the architecture of the two capital cities of the Tang Dynasty not only in architectural layout and decoration, but also in architectural technology.

3. Ancient Greek and Roman Cultural Factors in Henan Fine Arts

Glass was first invented about 5,000 years ago in the Mesopotamian Plain, then spread to Egypt, Greece, Rome, and through Central Asia to ancient China. In 1987, a complete yellow-green, long-necked glass bottle was unearthed from a tomb of the Han Dynasty in the eastern suburb of Luoyang. It was a typical Roman stirred-tire blown glass with white stripes revolving from the bottle's mouth edge to the bottom; its color is bright, and its shape elegant. In addition to Luoyang, similar glass wares have been found in Guangdong, Guangxi, Shandong, and Hebei Province. In the early twentieth century, George Croft, a Canadian, purchased from a tomb robber a Western glass bottle which was unearthed from an ancient tomb in Henan Province. Unlike the glass bottles found in the previously mentioned areas, on this glass bottle there are head portraits similar to that of Greek warriors, which proves more positively the origin of the ancient Greek style of the glass bottle.

In the mid-20th century, a small number of dragonfly eye glass beads(fig. 3−4) were unearthed from a tomb of the Warring States Period at Zhongzhou Road, Luoyang. These beads were made of glass with ring-shaped chromatography technology, looking like the dragonfly eye glass beads that flourished from the 6th Century B.C. to the 3rd Century B.C. in Egypt, Phoenicia and other eastern Mediterranean countries. Similarly, some soda-lime dragonfly-eye glass beads were also unearthed in the No.1 ancient tomb in Hougudui, Gushi County, in the ancient tomb in Xujialing, Xichuan County, Henan Province, and in the ancient tombs of the Warring States Period in Shandong, Guangdong, and Hubei provinces, which might be evidence of the opening of the Maritime Silk Road. That the Bronze Ding of the late Western Zhou Dynasty unearthed in Luoyang was inlaid with glass beads suffices to prove that China had mastered the western Asian glass making

图3-5 洛阳金村出土战国晚期铜镜
Fig. 3-5 A bronze mirror of the late Warring States Period unearthed in Jincun Village, Luoyang

背面骑马图像材料出土。

　　裸体雕塑是古希腊、罗马艺术中的一种常见主题，虽然裸体雕塑在公元前8000年至公元前5000年的法国、西班牙以及南欧草原的一些沿线国家，包括中国的红山文化中都有发现，但在进入文明历史时期以后，尤其是以儒家文化立国的两汉，裸体艺术是极为罕见的，也是不被世俗社会所允许的，但在河南却发现了一些两汉时期的裸体艺术的图像，如河南南阳汉代画像石上有裸体舞的图像，河南济源泗涧沟西汉晚期墓葬出土的一件绿釉陶树座上发现有裸体人雕塑。这种裸体图像不仅在河南被发现，在新疆和田、尉犁、民丰汉墓以及山东嘉祥、曲阜的画像石墓葬中皆有发现，这说明古希腊、罗马的裸体艺术图像可能通过"绿洲丝绸之路"传播到两汉时期的中国。

　　忍冬纹是古希腊的一种常见纹饰，流行于古希腊和罗马，约在北朝时期经由中亚、印度随着佛教文化传入中国，大量存在于佛教石窟寺艺术之中。洛阳龙门石窟火烧洞、莲花洞、魏字洞以及洛阳北魏永熙二年墓出土墓志、洛阳出土北魏晚期石碑座、北魏升仙棺皆发现了忍冬纹的身影，

technology.

Images of outings on horse and carriage were common in paintings of the Han Dynasty. They first appeared in the late Western Han Dynasty and prevailed during the Eastern Han Dynasty. At present, side images and three-quarters side images are mostly seen in the unearthed images of horses and carriages, while front images of horses and carriages, front and back images of horse riding are quite rare. For example, a bronze mirror of the late Warring States Period (fig. 3−5) unearthed in Jincun Village, Luoyang, Henan Province has a molded front image of horse riding; in a Han Dynasty brick unearthed in Xinye County, Nanyang, Henan Province was carved the front image of horse riding. In addition to Henan, the front riding images were also found in Jining and Tengzhou of Shandong Province. Pictures of back or front images of horse riding were common in ancient Greece and Central Asia of the Hellenistic Era, but were rarely seen in ancient China prior to the Han Dynasty. In fact, relics with the front and back images of horse riding were unearthed somewhere along the "Eurasian Prairie Silk Road" and "Oasis Silk Road" by which ancient Greek and Roman art spread eastward.

Nude sculptures were popular in ancient Greek and Roman art, although they were also found in France, Spain and countries along the southern European grasslands dating back to between 8000 B.C. and 5000 B.C. as well as in Chinese Hongshan Culture, they were extremely rare and unacceptable by the secular society, especially during the two Han Dynasties of China when the value of Confucianism became dominant. Nevertheless, some nude images of the two Han Dynasties were found in Henan, such as the nude dancer portraits on the Han Dynasty stone reliefs in Nanyang, Henan Province, and on a green-glazed pottery tree seat unearthed from a tomb of the late Western Han Dynasty in Sijiangou, Jiyuan County, Henan Province. As a matter of fact, nude images were also found in the Han Dynasty tombs in Hetian, Yuli and Minfeng of Xinjiang Province, and in the tombs with stone reliefs in Jiaxiang and Qufu of Shandong Province, which shows that art of nude sculpture in ancient Greece and Rome might have spread to China during the two Han Dynasties through the "Oasis Silk Road".

The honeysuckle pattern, common in ancient Greece, and popular in ancient Greece and Rome, was introduced to China together with Buddhist culture via Central Asia and India during the Northern Dynasties, and could be seen in the art

这些忍冬纹的发现佐证了古希腊艺术在河南的传播。

4.河南美术中所发现的胡人图像

在战国至汉代早期的汉语语义中，"胡人"指的是匈奴人，后来慢慢发展成对中国北方和西方的外族或外国人的泛称。自商代至汉唐以来的历史文献以及考古材料中发现了大量描述或者描绘胡人的文字和图像，主要集中在新疆、陕西、山西、河南、河北、山东、江苏等地，这些记录胡人的文字和图像反映了中原王朝与周边外族或外国交往的历史事实。河南地区所发现的胡人图像主要集中在洛阳、南阳、安阳等地区，如洛阳金村汉墓出土的画像砖射鹿图、南阳七孔桥画像石墓、南阳英庄画像石墓、南阳十里铺汉墓出土画像石、南阳王寨画像石墓、南阳东关李相公庄许阿瞿画像石墓、南阳方城杨集汉墓出土东汉"胡奴门"中皆发现了胡人图像。这些胡人图像有着典型的深目高鼻、满腮胡须的特征，头戴尖帽，左衽编发，身着胡服。

除画像石以外，自魏晋南北朝、隋唐以来，胡人图像还见于墓室壁画、卷轴画、瓷器之上。洛阳所发掘的唐安国相王孺人壁画墓（图3-6）、洛

图3-6 唐安国相王孺人壁画墓壁画 摄影：李伟年、何迎涛、周畅
Fig. 3-6 Tomb murals of Lord Xiang's imperial concubines of the Tang Dynasty

of most Buddhist grotto temples. For instance, in Luoyang, honeysuckle patterns were found in the Huoshao Cave, the Lotus Cave and the Weizi Cave of Longmen Grottoes, on the epitaph excavated from the tomb of the second year of the Yong Xi era of the Northern Wei Dynasty, on the stele pedestal of the later years of the Northern Wei Dynasty, and on the unearthed coffins of the Northern Wei Dynasty with pictures on them describing the process of becoming an immortal. The discovery of these honeysuckle patterns proves the spread of ancient Greek art throughout Henan Province.

4. Images of the Hu People Discovered in the Fine Arts of Henan

In China, from the Warring States Period to the early Han Dynasty, the "Hu People" referred to the Huns. Later it gradually developed to be a general term for minorities from northern and western China or foreigners. A large number of texts and images depicting the Hu people have been found in historical documents and archaeological materials from the Shang to the Han and the Tang Dynasties. They were mainly found in Xinjiang, Shaanxi, Shanxi, Henan, Hebei, Shandong, and Jiangsu provinces. These texts and images about the Hu people reflect the historical facts of the communication between the Central Plains dynasties and the neighboring foreign ethnicities and countries. The portraits of Hu people discovered in Henan Province are mainly located in Luoyang, Nanyang, and Anyang, such as those in the deer hunting pictures imprinted in the bricks unearthed from the tombs of the Han Dynasty in Jincun Village, Luoyang, the portrait stone tombs in Qikong Bridge Village, Yingzhuang Village, Wangzhai village, Xu Aqu's portrait stone tomb in Li Xianggong Village of Dongguan, Nanyang, portrait stones unearthed from Han Dynasty tombs in Shilipu of Nanyang, and "Gate with Hun Slave Portrait" unearthed from the tomb of the Han Dynasty in Yangji Village of Fangcheng. These images of the Hu people are typically bearded, with deep eyes, a high nose, braided hair, wearing a pointed hat and the Hu costume with the right piece of clothing being hidden to the left.

Since the Wei, Jin, Southern and Northern Dynasties, the images of the Hu people have also been seen in tomb murals, scroll paintings and porcelain. For instance, the images of the Hu people walking alone, or walking with (a) camel(s), were discovered in the tomb mural of Lord Xiang's imperial concubines of the Tang Dynasty excavated in Luoyang (fig. 3–6), and that of Ms. Doulu, the imperial

阳市郊唐睿宗豆卢氏壁画墓中皆绘有胡人图像，或独行站立，或牵骆驼。此外，在洛阳还发现有胡人俑的北魏墓葬十余座、隋唐墓葬五十余座，如北魏元邵墓、郭定兴墓，唐李嗣本墓、安菩夫妇墓等，在这些墓葬中出土了大量胡人俑（图3-7）。北魏孝文帝迁都洛阳后，国家实力增强，许多西域游牧部落归附，大量胡商进入洛阳。隋唐时期的洛阳不仅是丝绸之路的东起点，更是水陆交通的枢纽，逐渐发展成为国际性的大都市。在其全盛时期，四方纳贡，百国来朝，盛极一时。此时的洛阳是中外人士汇聚之地，也是文化交流的中心。胡人将西域风俗和文化艺术带入了黄河流域，使河洛地区的文明呈现出新的艺术风貌。

图3-7 胡人俑　摄影：何迎涛、周畅、李伟年
Fig. 3-7 Figurines of the Hu people unearthed in ancient tombs of Luoyang

除洛阳外，安阳、三门峡等地都发现过胡人俑。安阳，古称邺城，曾是曹魏、东魏、北齐时期的都城。北朝时期，随着中国和西域各国文化的频繁交流，在墓葬中用胡人充当出行仪仗以显示排场的现象蔚然成风。因此安阳地区也发现了较多的胡人俑，如北齐和绍隆墓、北齐范粹墓、梅元庄隋墓、桥村隋墓、张盛隋墓等。

值得注意的是安阳北齐范粹墓出土过一个黄釉乐舞扁壶（图3-8），

concubine of Emperor Rui Zong of the Tang Dynasty in Luoyang. Besides, in over 10 tombs of the Northern Wei Dynasty and over 50 of the Sui and Tang Dynasties were discovered a large number of figurines of the Hu people (fig. 3-7), such as the Yuan Shao Tomb, the Guo Dingxing Tomb of the Northern Wei Dynasty, and the Li Siben Tomb, the Mr. & Mrs. An Pu's Tomb of the Tang Dynasty. After Emperor Xiaowen of the Northern Wei Dynasty moved the capital city to Luoyang, the overall strength of the nation gradually increased, which pushed many western nomadic tribes to be under its governance, allowing many Hu merchants to flow to Luoyang. At the time, as the eastern starting point of the ancient Silk Road, and the hub of waterborne and land transportation, Luoyang in the Sui and Tang Dynasties gradually developed to be an international metropolis. In its heyday, Luoyang stood out as a center of cultural communication open to foreigners. Meanwhile, the capital city received loads of tributes rendered by its tributaries on a regular basis from all directions. In this context, the Hu people brought the customs and arts from the Western Regions into the Yellow River Basin, adding a new sense of art to the Heluo Civilization.

As a matter of fact, the Hu figurines were also found in Anyang, Sanmenxia and other places. Anyang, Yecheng City in ancient time, was once the capital city of the Wei State in the period of the Three Kingdoms, Eastern Wei and Northern Qi Dynasties. As a result of frequent cultural exchanges between China and the Western Regions countries, it was fashionable to have grand displays of Hu people as guarding warriors in the tombs in the Northern Dynasties. Many Hu figurines were discovered in Anyang, such as in the He Shaolong Tomb, Fan Cui Tomb of the Northern Qi Dynasty, Zhang Sheng Tomb of the Sui Dynasty, and the tombs of the Sui Dynasty in Mei Yuanzhuang Village, Qiaocun Village.

It is worth noting that on the yellow-glazed flattened pot unearthed from the Fan Cui Tomb of the Northern Qi Dynasty in Anyang (fig. 3-8), there is a molded scene featuring the Hu people dancing with music. On the front middle of the flattened pot stands a Hu dancer performing the "Hu Teng Dance", and above the dancer grows the "Life Tree" worshipped by the Sogdian with four figures playing musical instruments around him. Such kind of yellow-glazed flattened pots originated from the leather bag used by people in the Eurasian grassland. After being introduced to the Central Plains in the Northern Dynasties, these kinds of flattened

扁壶上刻画了胡人进行乐舞表演的情景。扁壶正面中间是一个跳胡腾舞的胡人，其上方是粟特人崇拜的生命树，周围四人似在表演乐器。这种黄釉扁壶的造型源自欧亚草原民族所使用的皮囊，它在北朝时期传入中原地区，不仅见于陶瓷中，还见于一些金银器具中。

　　这些深目高鼻的胡人是东西方贸易及艺术交流的参与者，他们活跃在社会各个领域，其身影随处可见，无论是宴乐百戏、骑马狩猎，还是从军、经商、出仕，胡人的生活面既广泛又深入。这些胡人作为一个个活生生的文化主体出现在汉人的生活圈中，才使得汉地工匠和艺术家在对其观察入微、认识深刻的基础上有所创作。胡人的形象被塑造成各种陶俑，甚至以镇守护卫的形象出现在墓葬之中。它们既象征着各族归顺臣服之心，又显示着墓主不同凡响的身份。在这些出土胡俑的墓葬中，墓主人除了是少数民族之外，还有明确记载来自域外国家的，他们的国别和族属从某种程度上也能反映出中西交流的广度和深度。

图3-8 安阳北齐范粹墓出土黄釉乐舞扁壶

Fig. 3-8 The yellow-glazed flattened pot unearthed from the Fan Cui Tomb of the Northern Qi Dynasty in Anyang

pots were seen not only on ceramics, but also on some gold and silver wares.

These deep eyed and high nosed Hu people participated in trade and art exchanges between the east and the west. They were so active in all social areas, extensively and deeply involved in every aspect of life, in the feast receptions and folk performances, horse riding and hunting, in military service and business, or being officials. This helped the Han craftsmen and artists know well of them and create these delicate Hu figurines. The images of the Hu people were molded into a variety of pottery figurines, including the guardian figurines that symbolized the minorities' loyalty and demonstrated the nobility of the tomb owners. Some of the unearthed tomb owners are minorities, some are foreigners explicitly recorded in documents. To some extent, their national or racial identities reflect the breadth and depth of communication between China and the West.

5. Western Asian Culture in the Fine Arts of Henan

In about 2000 B.C., wheat, sheep and cattle that originated in Western Asia were brought to the Central Plains through Central Asia and the Hexi Corridor. The discovery of wheat, sheep and cattle at the Erlitou Site in Luoyang indicates that back in the Erlitou Culture period, Luoyang had started material exchanges with Western and Central Asia. When the Han government dispatched Zhang Qian as an envoy to the Western Regions and later Ban Chao was dispatched to the Western Regions by Emperor Ming of the Eastern Han Dynasty, the relationship between the Central Plains and Western Asia was further developed. From the Northern Dynasties to the Sui and Tang Dynasties, this connection grew closer, which can be seen in the discovered works of art with Western Asian cultural factors, such as the images of lions, mythical winged beasts, bead-array patterns of decoration, and so on.

From the Han and Tang Dynasties to the Ming and Qing Dynasties, "lion" was written as "shi zi", the transliteration of the ancient Persian. It was also known as "suan ni", the transliteration of Scythian. Lions were native to Africa and later introduced to China when Zhang Qian was dispatched as an envoy to the Western Regions. Though not originally from China, the images of lions were widespread throughout ancient China, and are still popular today. For example, the lion dance, a part of traditional Chinese culture, is regarded as a cultural symbol by oversea Chinese in celebrating important festivals and events. As the eastern starting point of the Silk Road, a large number of ancient lion statues have been retained in Henan Province,

5. 河南美术中的西亚文化元素

在公元前 2000 年左右，发源于西亚的小麦、绵羊、黄牛经过中亚、河西走廊传入中原地区。洛阳二里头遗址发现小麦、绵羊和黄牛说明二里头文化时期洛阳已经与西亚、中亚有了物质方面的交流。张骞凿空西域，班超复通西域，中原地区和西亚之间的联系进一步加深。北朝至隋唐时期，这种联系愈加密切，反映在美术领域就是出现了大量带有西亚文化元素的艺术品，比较有代表性的包括狮子造型、有翼神兽、连珠纹饰等。

"狮子"在汉唐至明清期间皆写为"师子"，也被称作"狻猊"。"师子"为古波斯语的音译，"狻猊"则是斯基泰语的音译。狮子原产于非洲，大约在张骞通西域后传入中国。中国并不出产狮子，但狮子形象却在古代中国普遍存在并流行至今，舞狮更成为中华传统文化的一部分，在海外也成为华裔重要节庆活动中有代表性的文化符号。河南作为丝绸之路东方段的起点，留存了大量的古代狮子造型，如唐太子李弘恭陵墓石狮子、五代后晋石敬瑭显陵墓石狮子，以及巩义宋宣祖永安陵、宋太祖永昌陵、宋太宗永熙陵、宋真宗永定陵、宋仁宗永昭陵、宋英宗永厚陵、宋神宗永裕陵、宋哲宗永泰陵前的石狮子。明清以来，石狮子更是普及至一般的官僚及士绅、地主家庭门户前，成为中国传统民居文化极为常见的习俗。

有翼神兽在中国古代文物中是一种使用材料很广、流行时间很长的艺术形象。这一形象包括若干种类，比如带翼的狮、虎、鹿、羊等，其中尤以天禄、辟邪最为引人注目。有翼神兽的艺术形象（图 3-9）起源于西亚地区，且遍布于中亚、欧亚草原以及古代中国。河南出土发现了大量的有翼神兽，如新郑李家楼郑公大墓出土的莲鹤方壶上的有翼神兽、南阳宗资汉墓出土有翼神兽、洛阳孙旗屯出土辟邪（图 3-10）、洛阳偃师汉墓出土辟邪、洛阳伊川汉墓出土辟邪、洛阳孟津平乐出土辟邪、偃师高龙出土辟邪、偃师南蔡庄西晋陵出土有翼神兽（虎）、孟津油坊村出土北魏有

such as the stone lions in Gongling Mausoleum of Prince Li Hong of the Tang Dynasty, Xianling Imperial Mausoleum of Shi Jingtang of the Later Jin Dynasty of the Five Dynasties, and the stone lions at the gate of the Imperial Mausoleums of the Song Dynasty in Gongyi, including Yong'an Imperial Mausoleum of Emperor Xuan Zu, the Yongchang Imperial Mausoleum of Emperor Tai Zu, the Yongxi Imperial Mausoleum of Emperor Taizong, the Yongding Imperial Mausoleum of Emperor Zhenzong, the Yongzhao Imperial Mausoleum of Emperor Renzong, the Yonghou Imperial Mausoleum of Emperor Yingzong, the Yongyu Imperial Mausoleum of Emperor Shenzong, the Yongtai Imperial Mausoleum of Emperor Zhezong. Since the Ming and Qing Dynasties, stone lions were quite often seen in front of the houses of low-ranked officials, gentry and landlord families, and remained a very common custom in traditional Chinese residential culture.

Mythical winged beasts, an artistic image in ancient Chinese relics made of a variety of materials, were quite popular for a long time. This image includes several sub-categories, such as winged lions, tigers, deer, sheep, etc., among which Tianlu and Bi'xie (two mythical auspicious beasts in traditional Chinese sacrifice rituals) are the most remarkable. The artistic images of mythical winged beasts(fig. 3-9) originated in Western Asia and then spread all over Central Asia, the Eurasian grasslands and ancient China. Taking Henan as an example, a large number of mythical winged beasts have been unearthed, such as the ones on the rectangular pot intertwined with lotus and crane unearthed from the big tomb of Lord Zheng in the Spring and Autumn Period in Lijialou Village, Xinzheng, the mythical winged beasts in the tomb of Zong Zi from the Han Dynasty in Nanyang, and the tomb in Sunqitun Village of Luoyang(fig. 3-10), Bi'xie in the tombs of the Han Dynasty in Yan Shi County and Yichuan County, Luoyang, Bi'xie unearthed in Pingle Village of Mengjin County and Gaolong of Yanshi County, tigers unearthed from the Western Jin Mausoleum in South Caizhuang of Yanshi County, Bi'xie from the Northern Wei Dynasty in Youfang Village of Mengjin County and flying horses and lions in the Gong Mausoleum of the Tang Dynasty in Yanshi County. The art of mythical winged beasts was introduced to ancient China during the Warring States Period and prevailed throughout the two Han Dynasties, Wei, Jin, Southern and Northern Dynasties, the Sui and Tang Dynasties to the Northern Song Dynasty. For example, lots of mythical winged beasts, including Horn Rui (an auspicious beast with wings

翼神兽（辟邪）、偃师唐恭陵有翼神兽（飞马、狮子）。这种有翼神兽的艺术形象大约于战国时期传入古代中国，流行于两汉魏晋南北朝和隋唐，直至北宋时期仍然流行，河南巩义"七帝八陵"中就有大量的有翼神兽，

图3-9 西亚地区发现的有翼神兽
Fig. 3-9 The mythical winged beasts discovered in Western Asia

图3-10 洛阳博物馆藏孙旗屯出土东汉辟邪　摄影：何迎涛
Fig. 3-10 Bi'xie of Eastern Han Dynasty unearthed in Sunqitun Village, on display in Luoyang Museum

and horns), winged lions and the steles of Rui (an auspicious bird with a beast's head that symbolizes good luck) were discovered in the 8 royal cemeteries of 7 emperors of the Northern Song Dynasty in Gongyi, Henan. What needs to be mentioned is the Rui stele discovered in the Mausoleums of the Northern Song Dynasty in Gongyi. It was named Rui, but it is actually senmurv in ancient Persian art.

Originated from Sassanian Persia, the patterns of bead-array as a kind of decoration introduced to China during the Northern Dynasties and popular due to the development of Buddhist art, are widely used in brocades, gold and silver utensils, porcelain, lacquer wares, epitaphs, stone carvings and bricks, etc. They are characteristic in that small circles are joint to make larger ones, usually organized in four ways: scattering, joint horizontally or vertically, or the four sides joined in the four corners; they can be shaped in symmetrical images or a sole image, though the former is more popular. The patterns of bead-array are usually used in combination with other patterns, like that of curling grass, lotus, honeysuckle, reincarnating lotus, beast faces, etc., or they are used with images of birds, beasts, livestock or human beings in the center of the pattern. In Henan Province, the joint beads patterns are found mainly in Buddhist grotto arts, eaves tiles, porcelain, gold and silver wares, like the eaves tiles unearthed from the Yongning Temple, Luoyang (fig. 3−11), the niche and lower niches on the northern wall in Guyang Cave of Longmen Grottoes, and the backlight of the Yang Dayan Statue, in Guyang Cave of Longmen Grottoes, the yellow-glazed flattened pot unearthed from the Fan Cui Tomb of the Northern Qi Dynasty in Anyang, the rectangular bricks unearthed in the palace of the Sui and Tang Dynasties in Luoyang, etc.

6. The Art of Buddhist Statues in Henan Province

Indian Buddhism was introduced to the Central Plains around the time of the two Han Dynasties, but the art of Buddhist statues entered the Central Plains much later, and it entered in the middle and lower reaches of the Yangtze River around the two Jin Dynasties and began to flourish in the north during the Northern Dynasties. It was first introduced into Xinjiang through the "Oasis Silk Road" and then from there into the Hexi Corridor. When the Northern Wei Dynasty captured Liangzhou, and robbed it of 30,000 households and thousands of monks into Pingcheng (now Datong, Shanxi Province), the art of Buddhist statues was brought to the city and began to prosper in Henan Province since the Northern Wei Dynasty moved its

如有翼角瑞、有翼狮子、兽首瑞禽碑等。需要提及的是瑞禽碑，瑞禽碑在巩义宋陵中皆有发现，过去命名为"瑞禽"，实际上此"瑞禽"为古代波斯艺术中常见的"森木鹿"。

连珠纹饰源自波斯萨珊，是波斯萨珊艺术中一种常见的装饰纹样，大约在北朝时期传入中国，因佛教艺术而变得十分盛行，艺术载体遍及织锦、金银器、瓷器、漆器、墓志、石雕、砖瓦等。连珠纹的特征是小圆相连接组成一个大圆，其排列方式主要有四种：一为散点排列，二为横排相连，三为竖排相连，四为四面相连。构图方式或单独或对称，对称样式更多见。连珠纹多与其他纹饰相结合出现，如与卷草纹、莲花纹、忍冬纹、莲花化生纹、兽面纹等纹饰进行组合，或中间填饰鸟类、走兽、家畜、人物。河南所发现的连珠纹饰主要集中在佛教石窟、瓦当、瓷器、金银器上，如洛阳永宁寺出土的连珠莲花纹瓦当（图3-11）、龙门石窟古阳洞北壁龛楣和下层龛、龙门石窟古阳洞杨大眼造像背光、安阳北齐范粹墓出土的黄釉扁壶、洛阳隋唐宫城出土的方砖等。

图3-11 洛阳永宁寺出土连珠莲花纹瓦当　摄影：何迎涛

Fig. 3-11 The bead-array and lotus-patterned eaves tiles unearthed from the Yongning Temple, Luoyang

capital to Luoyang, which can be seen in the construction of Buddhist temples and grotto temples.

It has been documented that there were at least 3 Buddhist temples in Luoyang in the time of the Eastern Han Dynasty and the Wei State of the Three Kingdoms Period, and this number increased to 42 at the end of the Western Jin Dynasty. Then after the Northern Wei Dynasty moved its capital to Luoyang, the number of Buddhist temples there reached 1,367 which decreased to 45 during the Sui and Tang Dynasties, yet there were 271 Buddhist temples in total throughout Henan Province. After the Northern Wei Dynasty moved its capital to Luoyang, grotto temples in Henan Province had been excavated mainly in Luoyang, Anyang, Jiaozuo, etc. The grotto temples in Luoyang mainly include Longmen Grottoes in Luoyang City, Pugou Grottoes in Songxian County, Shuiquan Grottoes in Yanshi County, Wanfoshan Grottoes in Jili District, Xiejiazhuang Grottoes in Mengjin County, Stone Buddha Temple Grottoes in Yichuan County, Hutousi Grottoes in Yiyang County, Xiwo Grottoes in Xin'an County, etc., while those in Anyang include Xiaonanhai Grottoes, Lingquan Temple Grottoes, Stone Buddha Grottoes, cliffside statues in the Shuanglong Temple of Linzhou County, etc. In Jiaozuo, there are Shifotan Cliffside Statues in Bo'ai County and Xuangu Mountain Cliffside Statues in Qinyang City.

The art of Buddhist statues in Henan Province is represented by those of the Northern Dynasty, the Sui and Tang Dynasties, and the Northern Song Dynasty, covering the statues of Amitabha Buddha, Avalokitesvara, Sakyamuni, Bodhisattva, Maitreya Buddha, Ksitigarbha Bodhisattva (Ksitigarbha is a transcendent bodhisattva of Mahayana Buddhism. He is one of the most popular of the iconic bodhisattvas, especially in East Asia, where he often is called upon to guide and protect deceased children), Bhaisajyaguru Buddha (the Medicine Buddha who is venerated in much of Mahayana Buddhism because of his power of healing, both physical and spiritual), Udayana (a king of the city of Kaushambi in north-central India and a patron of Sakyamuni Buddha. He converted to the Buddha's teaching at the urging of his wife), Vairocana Buddha , Prabhutaratna (Abundant Treasures), meditators, the Heavenly Kings, Heroes, involving beliefs in Saddharma Pundarika Sutra (or the Sanskrit Lotus Sutra, regarded as one of the earliest examples of Mahayana Buddhist texts), Maitreya Pure Land (the Tusita Pure Land, also known as the Inner Court

6. 河南的佛教造像艺术

印度佛教大约在两汉之际传入中原，但佛教造像艺术传入中原却要晚得多，大约在两晋时期传入长江中下游地区，并在北朝时期开始在北方地区兴盛。印度佛教造像艺术通过"绿洲丝绸之路"传入新疆，然后由新疆传入河西走廊，北魏攻占凉州后将凉州三万户吏民和数千僧人掠至平城（今山西大同），由此河西佛教造像艺术传入平城。河南地区佛教造像艺术的兴盛始于北魏迁都洛阳，主要表现在兴建佛寺与石窟寺方面。

据文献记载，东汉、曹魏时期的洛阳至少有3座佛寺，到西晋末年（307–318）洛阳的佛寺增至42座，北魏迁都洛阳后洛阳的佛寺达到了1 367座，隋唐时期洛阳佛寺的数量有所减少，仅有45座，但整个河南地区的佛寺有271座。河南石窟寺的开凿主要是在北魏迁都洛阳以后，石窟寺主要集中在洛阳、安阳、焦作等地区。洛阳地区的石窟寺有龙门石窟、嵩县铺沟石窟、偃师水泉石窟、吉利区万佛山石窟、孟津谢家庄石窟、伊川石佛寺石窟、宜阳虎头寺石窟、新安西沃石窟等。安阳地区的石窟寺有小南海石窟、灵泉寺石窟、石佛洞窟、林州双龙寺摩崖造像等。焦作地区有博爱县石佛滩摩崖造像、沁阳市悬谷山摩崖造像。

河南佛教造像艺术以北朝、隋唐、北宋时期的佛教造像为主，造像题材涉及阿弥陀佛、观音、释迦、菩萨、弥勒佛、地藏、药师佛、优填王、卢舍那、多宝、思维、天王、力士等，包含了法华信仰、弥勒净土信仰、西天净土信仰、观音信仰、千佛思想、禅观思想等，其整体艺术风貌从云冈石窟犍陀罗、笈多样式逐渐转向本土化，在继承某些印度佛教艺术风格的同时融入南北朝及唐代的审美风格，更加符合中国人的审美趣味。

河南佛教造像以洛阳龙门石窟最具代表性。龙门石窟位于洛阳市洛龙区伊河两岸的龙门山与香山上，与莫高窟、云冈石窟、麦积山石窟并称中国"四大石窟"。龙门石窟开凿于北魏孝文帝年间，之后经东魏、西魏、

of Tusita, a majestic, pure heaven within the three realms, where Maitreya Buddha is teaching the Dharma), Sukhavati Pure Land (Pure Land of Bliss, often translated as Pure Land), Avalokitesvara, and beliefs in Thousand Buddhas and Zen Thought, etc. The overall artistic style of the Buddhist statues was gradually localized from Gandhara and Gupta art in Yungang Grottoes by inheriting some Indian Buddhist styles and meanwhile blending them with the traditional aesthetics of the Southern and Northern Dynasties and Tang Dynasties, so as to make a better fit with Chinese art.

The most representative Buddhist statues in Henan are those in Longmen Grottoes located on Longmen Mountain and Xiangshan Mountain on the banks of the Yihe River in Luolong District, Luoyang. Longmen Grottoes are also crowned as one of the Four Great Grottoes in China along with the Mogao Grottoes, the Yungang Grottoes and the Maiji Mountain Grottoes. Emperor Xiaowen of the Northern Wei Dynasty firstly directed the construction of Longmen Grottoes. After that, the Longmen Grottoes were continuously constructed during the following 400 years from the Eastern and Western Wei Dynasties, to the Northern Qi Dynasty, the Sui and Tang Dynasties, the Five Dynasties, until the Song Dynasty. Now the scenery area is 1 km long, with 2,345 niches and over a hundred thousand statues. The statues in Longmen Grottoes of the Northern Wei Dynasty are represented by those in the Binyang Cave (fig. 3−12), which were influenced in style by the statues in Yungang Grottoes, featuring slender figures with long loose robes and large belts, demonstrating the style shifting from masculinity to feminine tenderness, and the clothing from thickness and simplicity to lightness and ornamentation. This shift was inevitable in the process of localization of Buddhism and the art of Buddhist statues when they were introduced to China. Once the new style of art of Buddhist statues was developed in the Central Plains, it began to spread outward from Luoyang to other places nearby, and in turn, exerted its influence on the art of Buddhist statues in Yungang Grottoes, and spread further westward and influenced the art of the grotto statues in Chang'an and the Hexi Corridor. In addition to statues of the Northern Dynasties, such as the Sakyamuni Buddha, Maitreya Buddha, Amitabha Buddha and Avalokitesvarain, statues of the Tang Dynasty in the Longmen Grottoes also covered those of Vairocana Buddha, Bhaisajyaguru Buddha, Mahāvairocana (He is hailed as the primordial Buddha of great purity and peace), Ratnasambhava (one

图3-12-1 宾阳中洞正壁坐像
Fig. 3-12-1 Seated Buddha on the main wall of the Middle Binyang Cave

图3-12-2 宾阳中洞正壁右侧菩萨、阿难像　摄影：周畅
Fig. 3-12-2 The statues of Bodhisattva and Ananda on the right of the main wall in the Middle Binyang Cave

图3-12-3 宾阳中洞正壁左侧迦叶、菩萨像　摄影：李伟年
Fig. 3-12-3 The statues of Kasyapa and Bodhisattva on the left of the main wall in the Middle Binyang Cave

of Five Meditation Buddhas of Vajrayana or Tantric Buddhism whose mandalas and mantras focus on developing equanimity and equality), Udayana, Ksitigarbha, Karma Marga, the Avalokitesvara with thousands of hands and eyes, the multi-armed Bodhisattva, the Western Pure Land and the Buddha ancestors, etc. The statues of the Tang Dynasty in Longmen Grottoes are exquisite and good-looking, the Buddha statues plump and graceful with smooth and loose clothing (fig. 3–13). By integrating the overall three-dimensional beauty of the statues with the fine parts of foreign culture, the art of the grotto statues promoted the traditional decorative artistic lining techniques to a new level, making the Chinese-style statue art unprecedentedly prosperous.

III. Music and Literature Exchanges

The Tang Dynasty was an age of music and poetry. Emperor Xuanzong of the Tang Dynasty, Lady Yang (Emperor Xuanzong's beloved concubine) and the ministers were all masters in music. A poet once described an imaginary imperial concert in the early 8th century on which Emperor Xuanzong was playing the Jie drum (a Chinese musical instrument), Lady Yang plucking at the strings of a Pipa made of fragrant wood, the emperor's brother, Prince Ning, piping the flute, and the court musician Zhang Yehu playing Konghou (a plucked string instrument), while He Huaizhi beating out the tune and Li Guinian playing Bili (the Tartar pipe).

According to historical records, Emperor Xuanzong of the Tang Dynasty excelled in playing the Jie drum, and Lady Yang was a master of Pipa. Jie drum, Pipa, and the other three musical instruments mentioned in the poem, Konghou, Bili and flute were all introduced to China via the Silk Road. It is generally believed that the prototype of the Jie drum was introduced from Central Asia and named after the ethnic minority Jie in western China. In 1980, a painted Hu figurine of the Tang Dynasty with thick beard, deep eyes and a high nose was unearthed from a tomb of the Tang Dynasty in South Caizhuang Village, Yanshi County, Luoyang. The figurine is waving his right hand as his left hand extends forward. In each hand of the figurine is there a hole which was originally designed for holding musical instruments. It's a pity that the instruments have decayed. Judging from his posture, he should be striking a Jie drum. This particular drum was introduced to

北齐、隋、唐、五代、宋等朝代连续大规模营造达400余年，南北长达1公里，今存窟龛2 345个，造像10万余尊。龙门石窟的北魏造像以宾阳洞为代表（图3-12），宾阳洞的造像受到了云冈石窟造像"秀骨清像""褒衣博带"风格的影响，造型由浑厚庄严的阳刚之气转向风骨秀丽的阴柔之貌，衣饰由厚重简约之风转向轻巧修饰之美。这是佛教及佛教造像传入古

图3-13-1 奉先寺卢舍那大佛像（全身） 摄影：何迎涛

Fig. 3-13-1 The statue of Vairocana Buddha in the Fengxian Temple

China around the time of the Northern Dynasties and rapidly became popular. The Tang people even called it "top of the eight Chinese musical instruments". It was said that in order to practice this drumming skill, Emperor Xuanzong of the Tang Dynasty stroked off three fully-loaded cabinets of rods. When it comes to the Pipa, its prototype originated from the Mesopotamian Basin and then gradually spread to China where it is known as Pipa, to France where it is known as lute, and to Spain where it is called guitar. Konghou is a variation of the western harp. Similar to Suona (a traditional Chinese musical instrument with distinctively loud and high-pitched sound), Bili originated in Persia. Flute was also known as "horizontal blowing" because similar musical instruments of the Han Dynasty were held vertically when being played while flute from the Western Regions was held horizontally. Although primitive flute existed in China a long time ago, this instrument grew popular in the Han Dynasty after the introduction of Central Asian music.

All in all, the poem mentioned above describes a band playing musical instruments from different part of the world. Since the opening of the Silk Road, Chinese music had been deeply influenced by foreign factors. This influence reached its peak during the Sui and Tang Dynasties. People then generally despised traditional music and were fond of the new Western Regions music, Yanyue (Yan Music) or "Vulgar Music". What is depicted in this poem is exactly the situation in which the Tang Dynasty people played Yanyue.

1. The Silk Road and Chinese Music during the Han and Wei Dynasties

At the time, Luoyang, the center of foreign music transmission, was steeped in an exotic atmosphere. The earliest music influenced by the Silk Road is "Melody of Drum, Horn, and Flute". The legend says that Zhang Qian brought back to China some musical instruments, such as flute and horn, from the Western Regions to be used in martial music. In the Eastern Han Dynasty, a formal rule was formed, which regulated that generals who commanded more than 10,000 soldiers were eligible to use this music as a guard of honor for battle. In 1965, pottery figurines (fig. 3−14) unearthed from the Yuan Shao Tomb in Luoyang confirmed the posture of playing "Melody of Drum, Horn and Flute": the valiant musicians rode on horseback while playing the drum, which is quite military in style. The owner of the tomb was the grandson of Emperor Xiaowen of the Northern Wei Dynasty, a senior general who died young at the age of 23. There are over 30 pieces of "Melody of Drum, Horn

代中国后本土化进程中出现的必然形貌,这种以"秀骨清像""褒衣博带"为主要特征的中原风格一经形成,便以洛阳为中心向外传播,反过来又影响了云冈石窟,同时亦西传并影响了长安及河西走廊地区的石窟造像艺术。龙门石窟的唐代造像题材,除北朝已有的释迦牟尼佛、弥勒佛、阿弥陀佛和观世音菩萨以外,又出现了卢舍那佛、药师佛、大日如来、宝生如来、优填王、地藏、业道、千手千眼观音、多臂菩萨、西方净土变和历代祖师像等。龙门石窟中的唐代造像(图3–13)精美、俊逸,佛像身躯丰满挺秀,衣纹疏朗流畅,在追求立体造型的同时,又融合了外来文化的精华,把传统的线条和装饰性的艺术手法提高到了一个新的层次,使具有中国风格的造像艺术空前鼎盛。

图3-13-2 奉先寺卢舍那大佛头部像　摄影:何迎涛

Fig. 3-13-2 The head of the statue of Vairocana Buddha in the Fengxian Temple

三、音乐、文学的交流与传播

"三郎老手打羯鼓,太真纤指弹龙香。箜篌野狐拍怀智,觱篥龟年

and Flute" recorded in literature passed down in history, one of which is "Luoyang Mo(On a Road in Luoyang)". The poetic genius Li Bai of the Tang Dynasty wrote lyrics for it: "Who's that young man with a fine face like jade? He has returned and crossed the Tianjin bridge. Appreciating flowers on the road of the East District, he became the attraction for Luoyang pedestrians."This song depicts a handsome young man Pan Yue who went to appreciate flowers in the east of Luoyang city and caused a sensation. Ladies and maidens along the way offered fruits to him to express their love. Probably such bold style folkway could only exist in the liberal environment of mixed ethnic inhabitants in Luoyang.

"Melody of Drum, Horn and Flute" appeared in the Han Dynasty and prevailed in the Wei, Jin, Southern and Northern Dynasties and remained throughout the Tang Dynasty. While it was declining, a new type of music was emerging. The concert in the poem mentioned at the beginning of this chapter represents a new age in which the music of the Western Regions influenced Chinese music deeply and rapidly developed to be the mainstream. Traditionally, Chinese music had always adopted the pentatonic scale. "Melody of Drum, Horn and Flute" of the Han and Wei Dynasties used vertical or horizontal flutes (Xiao or Di) to set the tune. In the late Northern Dynasties and the early Tang Dynasty, a group of Western musicians won over audience with Pipa music from the kingdom of Qiuci. Since then, a new form of music had become popular in China, which uses the heptatonic scale while using Pipa to set the tune, i.e. Yan Music.

2. Silk Road and Chinese music in the Northern Dynasties and Sui and Tang Dynasties

Cao Miaoda, a famous Pipa performer, was born in Luoyang City of the Northern Wei Dynasty, in a Sogdian family that was good at playing Qiuci music for generations. The family came from the Cao kingdom in Central Asia, so it took Cao as its surname. After the split of the Northern Wei, the two short-lived separatist dynasties of the Eastern Wei and Northern Qi were established with the city of Yecheng(now Anyang) as the center, and a large number of musical talents including the Cao family moved from Luoyang to the new capital Yecheng.

People in the Northern Qi Dynasty were zealous about music. That was the golden age of Western Regions musicians. The official and formal historical document, *Book of Sui: Music Record*, records that emperors of the Northern Qi

笛宁王。"

精通演奏羯鼓的唐玄宗亲自表演，杨贵妃用龙香木制成的拨子弹奏琵琶，宁王吹笛，张野狐弹箜篌，贺怀智击节为拍，李龟年弹觱篥。这是一场古代诗人想象中的公元8世纪前期的宫廷音乐会。唐代是诗歌与音乐的时代，唐玄宗和他的宠臣都擅长音乐。在上面的诗句里，唐玄宗、杨贵妃、皇帝的哥哥宁王，以及宫廷音乐家张野狐、贺怀智、李龟年各自演奏擅长的乐器，其乐融融。

史书记载，唐玄宗非常擅长演奏羯鼓，杨贵妃则是琵琶高手。羯鼓和琵琶，还有诗里提到的另外三种乐器——箜篌、觱篥和笛，都是通过丝绸之路传入中国。一般认为，羯鼓的原型来自中亚，因中国西部的少数民族羯族而得名。1980年，河南洛阳偃师市南蔡庄唐墓出土一件彩绘胡俑，人物造型高鼻深目，胡须茂密，左手前伸，右手挥舞。胡俑的手中有孔洞，原本是手执乐器的，可惜乐器已经朽坏。从姿态推测，他正在敲击的乐器便是羯鼓。这种乐器大约在北朝传入中国，并且迅速流行起来，唐人甚至把它称为"八音之领袖"，即一切乐器的首领。据说唐玄宗为了练习羯鼓演奏技艺，敲断的鼓杖可以装满三个立柜。琵琶的原型起源于两河流域，这一类型的乐器流传极广，传到中国叫琵琶，传到法国叫鲁特琴，传到西班牙叫吉他。箜篌是西方竖琴的变种。觱篥类似唢呐，起源于波斯。笛又名"横吹"，因为汉代流行的本土乐器排箫是竖着吹奏的，而来自西域的笛却是横向吹奏的。虽然中国很早就有原始的笛，但这种乐器的真正流行是在汉代中亚曲目传入以后。

总而言之，上面引用的四句诗描述了一支世界化的乐队。自从丝绸之路开通，中国音乐一直深受外来因素的影响，这种影响在隋唐时期达到高峰，人们普遍厌弃传统音乐，喜爱西域化的新式音乐，时人称之为燕乐或者俗乐。这首诗中描绘的，正是唐代演奏燕乐的情形。

Dynasty favored foreign music, "There are various kinds of music like Pi Dance of Xiliang, Qing Music and Qiuci. But since the Emperor Wen Xiang (Gao Yang, the first emperor of the Northern Qi Dynasty), people began to appreciate the performance of playing the flute, Pipa and Five-strings, and girls' singing and dancing. When it came to the Heqing era of the Northern Qi Dynasty (from 562 A.D. to 564 A.D.), these performances grew more popular. Gao Wei, the last emperor of the Northern Qi loved solely Hu music and indulged a lot in it." According to the record, although there coexisted many types of Chinese and Qiuci music in the Northern Qi Dynasty, Qiuci music represented by pear-shaped Pipa and the five-stringed Pipa was more popular and favored by the nobility. Emperor Gao Wei particularly loved Qiuci Pipa music. He often sang while playing the Pipa by himself and up to hundreds of people were there to accompany him, or he ordered Cao Miaoda to play the Pipa while he himself beat the drum in harmony with the music.

Because of the emperor's favor, a large number of musicians, headed by Cao Miaoda, were appointed senior generals. Under such enticement, some upper-class Han families also made their children learn to play the Pipa and the Xianbei language so as to cater to the preferences of the dignitaries. The Northern Qi Dynasty existed only 27 years, but its musician group was inherited by the later dynasties. Hu music was popular successively in the Northern Zhou Dynasty and the Sui Dynasty. In the Sui Dynasty, Cao Miaoda was assigned to participate in regulating musical tones. It was his efforts that made the heptatonic scale adopted as the basis of the musical mode in China.

The core spirit of Chinese culture is "rites and music". Music is regarded as an important tool for maintaining social order and cultivating a gentleman's character. In ancient China's historical legends, "regulating rituals and making music" are two of the major issues for the imperial kings. However, on the basis of the popular Hu music, the music system of the Sui Dynasty was thoroughly westernized. The folk music of the Sui Dynasty developed by Cao Miaoda used 5 gongs (corresponding to Do in the numbered musical notation) and 35 alternative types of scale. Later in the Tang Dynasty, it was simplified to 28 scales, then in the Song Dynasty further simplified to 7 gongs and 12 scales, and in the Yuan Dynasty there were only 6 gongs and 11 scales. Finally, in the Ming Dynasty 9 modes remained and were passed down

1、汉魏时期的丝绸之路与中国音乐

当时洛阳是外来音乐传播的中心,这座城市浸染着浓厚的异域之风。这里最早受到丝绸之路影响的音乐门类是"鼓角横吹曲"。相传张骞从西域带回横笛、号角等乐器,这些乐器被用来吹奏军乐;到了东汉时期,更形成正式的制度,规定统率万人以上的将军有资格使用此种乐曲作为出行的仪仗。1965 年洛阳元邵墓出土的奏乐陶俑(图 3-14),印证了"鼓角横吹曲"的演奏形态,英武的乐手骑在马背上击鼓奏乐,颇有军旅风姿。该墓墓主是北魏孝文帝的孙子,一位二十三岁早逝的高级将领。传世文献中记载的"鼓角横吹曲"约有三十多个曲目,其中一个曲目为《洛阳陌》,"诗仙"李白曾为它创作歌词:"白玉谁家郎,回车渡天津。看花东陌上,惊动洛阳人。"这首曲子描绘了这样的场景:潘岳去城东看花,他的英俊惊动了整个洛阳城,沿途妇女纷纷向他的车中投掷果子表达爱意。这样大胆热辣的民风,可能只有在洛阳多民族杂居的开放环境下才会出现。

"鼓角横吹曲"在汉代出现,盛行于魏晋南北朝,到唐代尚有遗风。在它渐渐衰落的同时,另一种新型的音乐形式正在兴起。本专题开篇诗歌里的那场音乐会,代表着一个崭新的时代。西域因素对中国音乐的影响更加深入,并且迅速发展为中国音乐的主流。传统上,中国音乐一直采用五声音阶。汉魏时期的"鼓角横吹曲"使用箫、笛定调。北朝后期到唐朝前期,一批西域音乐家用龟兹国传来的琵琶乐征服了听众,此后中国开始流行采用七声音阶、以琵琶定调的新型音乐形式——燕乐。

2、北朝、隋唐时期的丝绸之路与中国音乐

北魏洛阳城一个世代擅长演奏龟兹音乐的粟特家族,诞生了著名的琵琶演奏家曹妙达。这个家族来自中亚曹国,因此以曹为姓。 北魏分裂

to today. In other words, contemporary Chinese music is still being affected by this ancient musical style.

Besides, the court music of the Sui Dynasty was categorized into nine types: Qing music, Xiliang music, Qiuci music, Shule music, Kangguo music, Anguo music, Tianzhu music, Gaoli music and Libi music. Five of them (Qiuci music, Shule music, Kangguo music, Anguo music and Tianzhu music) were musics of the Western Regions. The Tang Dynasty inherited the music system of the Sui Dynasty, but slightly changed it. At that time, the court music was divided into ten types, adding to it Gaochang music, another kind of music from the Western Regions.

By the time of Emperor Xuanzong of the Tang Dynasty, Chinese music generally bore features of "Hu music" both in musical instruments and songs. The main Chinese bowed string instrument, Huqin fiddle (the predecessor of Hu Qin), was introduced to China at the end of the Tang Dynasty. Unlike the western violin, the Chinese Huqin has only two strings, a narrow range, and focuses on imitating human vocals. There is also the Yangqin(dulcimer), which is generally believed to have been introduced to China by sea in the late Ming Dynasty, but some other scholars believe that it was introduced by the Land Silk Road in the Tang Dynasty. All in all, most instruments of Chinese folk music nowadays have inherited some features of those from the Near East.

People in the Tang Dynasty had a great passion for foreign music. The poets in the mid Tang Dynasty portrayed the social customs of Luoyang at that time, saying that "Women are willing to marry men of the Western Regions and learn to dress in western ways, and musicians play music of the Western Regions", "Every family in Luoyang learns Hu music", and so on. This shows the popularity of foreign music at that time.

By the way, for the Sogdian family, Cao Miaoda's life experience was by no means an exceptional case. Hu music was popular in the Northern Dynasties and the Sui and Tang Dynasties. Many Hu people were appointed generals and many Sogdian musicians were appointed military officers. In 1981, An Pu and his wife's tomb was accidentally discovered in the east Longmen Mountains. It was the first tomb of foreign immigrants of the Tang Dynasty excavated scientifically in Luoyang, from which exquisite Tang Sancai utensils and Eastern Roman gold coins were unearthed. According to the epitaph, An Pu was a general who submitted to

图3-14 洛阳元邵墓出土的奏乐陶俑
Fig. 3-14 A pottery figurine striking up a tune unearthed from the Yuan Shao Tomb in Luoyang

以后,以邺城(今安阳)为中心建立了东魏和北齐两个短命的割据王朝,大量音乐人才从洛阳迁往新都邺城,曹家也在其列。

北齐时期,世人酷爱音乐,也是西域乐人的黄金时代。官修正史《隋书·音乐志》记载了北齐帝王对外来音乐的喜爱:"杂乐有西凉鼙舞、清乐、龟兹等。然吹笛、弹琵琶、五弦及歌舞之伎,自文襄(即北齐的开国皇帝高洋)以来,皆所爱好,至河清(北齐年号,562—564)以后,传习尤盛。后主唯赏胡戎乐,耽爱无已。"根据这则记载,虽然北齐时代同时存在中国本土和来自龟兹国的多种音乐,但以曲项琵琶、五弦琵琶为代表乐器的龟兹乐明显更为流行,也更受统治者欢迎。北齐后主高纬尤其喜爱龟兹琵琶乐,他常常要么"自弹胡琵琶而唱之,和者数百人",要么命令曹妙达弹奏琵琶,"自击胡鼓以和之"。

因为帝王的喜爱,以曹妙达为首的一大批乐人被任命为高级将领。

the Tang Dynasty, and An Jinzang, his only son and an officer in charge of music, enjoyed a great reputation in history. At that time, An Jinzang served as a music officer under Li Dan, the son of Emperor Wu Zetian. It was he who stood up and proved the prince's innocence by laparotomy when he was framed for rebellion and could not defend himself. For his bravery and loyalty, An Jinzang won great admiration from Chinese intellectuals.

3. The Evolution of Poetry and Music in the Background of the Silk Road

China is a country of verse, and those of the Tang, Song and Yuan Dynasties are especially brilliant. Each genre of these verses, poetry of the Tang Dynasty, ci of the Song Dynasty and drama (aria) of the Yuan Dynasty, has its own merits, but they are also common in that they are all musical literature. Yan Music in the Sui and Tang Dynasties contributed the most important poems of the prosperous Tang Dynasty, especially the seven-character quatrains, an important form of the poetry in the Tang Dynasty.

According to historical records, officers guarding the border dedicated six "frontier tunes" that were named after the frontier regions to Li Longji, Emperor Xuanzong of the Tang Dynasty who loved Hu music. According to the historical records, tunes in the Tianbao Era (742 A.D.–756 A.D.) were all named after the names of the border states, such as Liangzhou, Yizhou, Ganzhou and so on. The so-called "Daqu", a form of the music that originated in the most prosperous period of the Tang Dynasty, was very long, complex in structure, and required a large number of musicians, singers and dancers to cooperate. It was also the most advanced form of Yan Music during the Tang Dynasty.

During the Tang Dynasty, the lyrics for the Daqu were all verses of four lines of seven Chinese characters, that is, the seven-character quatrain. All the musics recorded in the history of the Tang Dynasty, such as Liangzhou, Yizhou, Ganzhou, Luzhou, Cupailuzhou and Shui Diao, used this kind of verse as lyrics. In turn, it was this fact that made the seven-character quatrain the most popular form of verse. As lyrics, the style of poetry is bound to be influenced by its music style. The six frontier Daqu are all Hu music with intense rhythm, logically, many poems, like *Lyric to Liangzhou* and *Tune to Yizhou*, are both intense, vigorous and exciting in emotion. Most of the lyricists of the frontier Daqu were famous frontier poets, such as Wang Changling, Wang Zhihuan, Gao Shi, Cen Sen and so on. It is obvious that the

在这样的诱惑下,一些汉族上层家庭也教导子弟学习琵琶和鲜卑语,以便迎合北齐显贵的喜好。北齐国祚只有短短 27 年,但是它的乐工群体却被之后的王朝继承,消灭北齐的北周王朝、夺取北周政权的隋王朝同样流行胡乐。在隋朝,曹妙达受命参加乐律的制定工作,在他的推动下,七声音阶被采纳为调式的基础。

中国文化的核心精神是"礼乐",音乐被看作维持社会秩序、塑造君子品格的重要工具。在中国古代历史传说中,"制礼作乐"是圣王最核心的事迹。在社会流行胡乐的基础上,隋代乐制彻底西域化了。曹妙达制定的隋俗乐使用五宫三十五调,唐代简化为二十八调,宋代继续简化为七宫十二调,元代简化为六宫十一调,明代最终简化为九个宫调,并流传至今。换言之,中国音乐至今仍受其影响。

不仅如此,隋代宫廷音乐被编制为"九部乐":清乐、西凉乐、龟兹乐、疏勒乐、康国乐、安国乐、天竺乐、高丽乐、礼毕乐。其中有五部(龟兹乐、疏勒乐、康国乐、安国乐、天竺乐)属于西域音乐。唐代因袭隋朝制度,略加改变,当时的宫廷音乐分为十部,增加了一种同样来自西域的高昌乐。

到唐玄宗时,中国音乐从乐器到曲目大多带有"胡乐"的基因。中国主要拉弦乐器胡琴的前身在唐末传入中国。和西方的提琴不同,中国胡琴只有两根弦,音域稍窄,侧重模仿人声。还有扬琴,这种乐器一般认为是在明末由海上传入中国,但也有学者认为它是在唐代由陆上丝绸之路传入中国。总而言之,现在中国民族音乐的大部分乐器也都具有近东血脉。

唐人酷爱外来音乐,中唐诗人描绘当时洛阳的社会风俗,有"女为胡妇学胡妆,伎进胡音务胡乐""洛阳家家学胡乐"等诗句,可见当时外来音乐流行的社会风气。

顺便一提,对粟特家族来说,曹妙达的人生经历绝非个例。北朝和隋唐时期流行胡乐,又喜欢以胡人为将,所以很多粟特音乐家都被任命为武官。1981 年,人们在洛阳龙门意外发现了安菩夫妇的墓葬。这是洛阳首座经过科学发掘的唐代外来移民墓葬,其中出土了精美的三彩器以及东

vigorous music of the Western Regions had shaped the vigorous poetic style in the Tang Dynasty.

Since Daqu required a lot of players to perform in cooperation, and after the Anshi Rebellion, the court's finances could not afford a huge band, it became very difficult to perform a whole Daqu. It was recorded that after the mid Tang Dynasty, the artists played only one segment of it on ordinary occasions.

But at that time in Luoyang, a new kind of music sprang up which was called by the famous poets Liu Yuxi and Bai Juyi as "new music in Luoyang". It is a kind of small and fresh tune like *Yang Liu Zhi*. A poem by Bai Juyi entitled *Yang Liu Zhi* depicts the beautiful scenery of Luoyang in spring, "Outside the gate of Tao Ling are several trees, and many willows in Yafu's military camp. But neither can match the east capital in February, when golden willows dangle along Luoyang bridge."

Although it was called "new music in Luoyang", *Yang Liu Zhi*, also called *Zhe Yang Liu* and played on flutes, was actually created in the Sui Dynasty, and regarded by people in the Tang Dynasty as a symbol of Luoyang. Both the two greatest poets in Chinese history, Li Bai and Du Fu, chanted the performance of it in Luoyang. Li Bai's *Hearing a Flute on a Spring Night in Luoyang* says, "From whose house comes the voice of flute of jade unseen? It fills the town of Luoyang, spreads by wind of spring. Tonight I hear the farewell song of Willow Green. To whom the tune will not nostalgic feeling bring?" Du fu's *Playing Flute* also says, "The willows in hometown now shake and lose their leaves, and their sorrow is full of this tune."

During the mid Tang Dynasty, this simple and melodious tune was loved by more people and stood out from a variety of Yuefu tunes to become the basis of the popular new music. Bai Juyi created *20 Rhymes of Yang Liu Zhi* in this way, and he wrote a note following the title, "*Yang Liu Zhi*, a new music in Luoyang that young girls in Luoyang are good at singing. Their gorgeous lyrics and beautiful melodies are very touching. Hence I write this in praising of them." The *Yang Liu Zhi* written by Bai Juyi and Liu Yuxi were still in the same form of four lines of seven characters as the lyrics of Daqu. But with the development of the music, the tune of *Yang Liu Zhi* also changed. Later, *Yang Liu Zhi* in Dunhuang Opera was in the form of long and short sentences, with its lyrics as follows:

Spring comes and goes, time and time again.

So do summer and winter.

罗马金币。根据墓志记载，安菩是一位归附唐朝的将军，他的独生子安金藏则是一位乐官。安金藏在历史上享有盛名，他在武则天之子李旦手下担任乐官时，恰逢李旦被人诬陷造反，无以自明，安金藏挺身而出，剖腹明志，以证明李旦的清白，他的勇敢和忠诚深受中国文人钦佩。

3. 丝路背景下的诗歌与音乐演化

中国是诗歌的国度，唐诗、宋词、元曲，"一代有一代之所胜"。而这几种诗体的共同点，就在于它们都是音乐的文学。隋唐燕乐造就了盛唐诗，尤其是唐诗最重要的一种体裁——七言绝句。

唐玄宗李隆基喜爱胡乐，守卫边境的官员献给他六支以边境州郡命名的边地大曲。史书记载，"天宝乐曲，皆以边地名，若《凉州》《伊州》《甘州》之类"。所谓"大曲"，是唐代音乐的一种组织形式，乐曲篇幅浩大、结构复杂，而且需要大量演员共同演奏、歌唱和舞蹈。边地大曲产生于唐朝最繁荣的时期，它也是唐朝燕乐最高级的形态。

唐代人给大曲谱写的歌词，一律采用七言四句的形式，也就是七言绝句。史书记载的唐代音乐《凉州》《伊州》《甘州》《陆州》《簇拍陆州》《水调》等，都用绝句作为歌词。反过来，七绝之所以成为最普遍的诗歌形式，也正是这个原因。因为是歌词，所以诗歌的风格必然会受音乐风格的影响。六支边地大曲都是音节激昂的胡乐，所以唐诗才会有那么多首亢爽刚健的《凉州词》《伊州曲》。边地大曲的词作者大多是边塞诗名家，比如王昌龄、王之涣、高适、岑参等。刚健雄浑的西域音乐，造就了刚健雄浑的盛唐诗风。

大曲需要众多艺人共同演奏，安史之乱之后，由于宫廷财力萎缩，难以继续维持庞大的乐队，也就很难演出完整的大曲。据记载，中唐以后普通场合演奏音乐，一般只选大曲的某个片段。

但同一时间，在洛阳又兴起了新的音乐。这种音乐被当时有名的诗人刘禹锡、白居易称为"洛下新声"，它是《杨柳枝》一类清新的小调。

Crescent to full moon is such a circle.

Day by day, we get old.

Only the time I spent in my yard is immortal,

while I have been dust and no longer sitting in my lounge.

This piece of lyric not only adds sounds and dictions, but also has linking words. The lyrics of Dunhuang Opera, as a record of folk music, indicate that the new musical form is more flexible than the complex and regular Daqu.

This kind of musical lyrics later developed and replaced the poetry of the Tang Dynasty to become Ci poetry of the Song Dynasty. Some tunes of Ci in the Song Dynasty originated from the frontier Daqu, such as *Liu Zhou Ge Tou*, *Shi Zhou Xing* and so on, but the most popular were the newly-created tunes like *Yang Liu Zhi* and *Yu Lin Ling*, etc. The early works of Ci available now are mainly "Lyrics to the Dunhuang Tunes" discovered in Dunhuang. This fact implies that after its emergence, the new musical form Ci spread westward along the Silk Road and influenced some areas on the Silk Road in reverse.

The mutual influence of the Silk Road runs through the history of Chinese music literature. Following Ci of the Song Dynasty, the verse form of the Yuan Dynasty is Qu which is similar to Ci in that it was developed from the former. Just like the poetry of the Tang Dynasty and Ci of the Song Dynasty, the verse form of the Yuan Dynasty is also a form of poetry. But at the same time, it is also a form of opera: a number of tunes are strung together in accordance with certain rules to form a drama. As a kind of music, Qu of the Yuan Dynasty was divided into the Northern Tune (usually in the heptatonic scale with its tune set by the Pipa with a fast rhythm) and the Southern Tune (usually in the pentatonic scale with its tune set by the flute with a slow rhythm), and the former was more popular than the latter.

The Northern Tune that had been popular since the Jin and Yuan Dynasties was sung in Henan dialect, namely "Zhongzhou Phonology", or "Heluo Zhengyin". Besides the phonology, the stories of the operas in the Song, Jin and Yuan Dynasties, especially those created before the late Yuan Dynasty, mostly occurred in Henan, especially in Kaifeng, Luoyang and Zhengzhou.

4. The Silk Road and Folk Art of Quyi

It is recorded in history that Li Longji lived a melancholy life after his abdication. In order to relieve his grief, the eunuch who waited on him summoned

白居易创作的一首《杨柳枝》描绘洛阳春天的美景:"陶令门前四五树,亚夫营里百千条。何似东都正二月,黄金枝映洛阳桥。"

虽然被称作"洛下新声",《杨柳枝》其实在隋朝就已创作出来。这支曲子又叫《折杨柳》,用笛子演奏。唐人把这首曲子看作洛阳的象征,中国历史上最伟大的两位诗人李白和杜甫都吟咏过洛阳人演奏它的情形。李白《春夜洛城闻笛》云:"谁家玉笛暗飞声,散入春风满洛城。此夜曲中闻折柳,何人不起故园情。"杜甫《吹笛》也说:"故园杨柳今摇落,何得愁中曲尽生。"

中唐时,这首结构简单、曲调缠绵的小曲,受到更多人的喜爱,它从各种乐府旧曲中脱颖而出,成为民间广泛流传的"新声"曲调的基础。白居易在这个风气下创作了《杨柳枝二十韵》,题下自注称:"《杨柳枝》,洛下新声也。洛之小妓有善歌之者,词章音韵,听可动人,故赋之。"白居易和刘禹锡填写的《杨柳枝》,格式仍然是七言四句,和以前大曲的格式相同。但是随着音乐的发展,作为词调的《杨柳枝》很快有了新的变化。后来敦煌曲中的《杨柳枝》,已是长短句格式,其词曰:

春去春来春复春,寒暑来频。

月生月尽月还新,又被老催人。

只见庭前千岁月,长在长存。

不见堂上百年人,尽总化微尘。

这首曲辞不仅有添声、加辞,而且还有衬字。敦煌曲是民间演唱的实录,歌词显示出新的音乐形式要比复杂、规范的大曲更加灵活。

这种小曲发展起来以后就是唐诗的替代者——宋词。宋词中也有源自边地大曲,从中缩减而来的《六州歌头》《石州行》等词牌,但是占主流的还是《杨柳枝》《雨霖铃》等新创的曲子。现在我们能够看到的早期词作,主要是在丝路重镇敦煌发现的"敦煌曲子词",这说明新兴的音乐形式"词"出现之后,沿着丝路向西传播,反向影响到丝绸之路上的一些地区。

丝绸之路的双向影响贯穿了整个中国音乐文学史。继宋词之后兴起

various folk performers to the court.

The Tang Dynasty is a crucial period for the development and maturity of Quyi art, whether magic, acrobatics or storytelling and singing. Then, these forms of art had already been in the early form of their later generations. These art forms are related to those of India and Iran. The acrobatic illusionists who came to China along the Silk Road can often be seen in the records of Chinese history books. Chinese people at that time thought that ancient Romans were masters of magical acrobatic art. On the bricks of the Han Dynasty unearthed in Xinye County, Henan Province, there is the image of a Hu person spitting fire. He has a high nose, deep eyes and a pointed hat. The book *Wei State* records that in Da Qin (Ancient Rome) "many citizens are acrobats or magicians, who can spit fire, tie and untie themselves, and juggle 12 balls, which look wonderful and fantastic". Here the art of fire spitting, ball juggling and rope jumping are the several most important kinds of Chinese acrobatics. Indian artists who came to China during the Tang Dynasty were also known for their skills in creating illusions. Records show that their skills were much similar to those of the Romans.

At the foot of Mount Funiu in Baofeng County, southwest in Henan Province, there is a village called Majie Village where a lively festival is held annually on the 13th, lunar January. At that time, thousands of Quyi artists from all over the country came to this humble village to perform their own unique art, competing for the "Championship of the Quyi Art" which is voted for by the audience. Some extremely rare and almost lost plays can often be seen there, and all these arts can be traced back to popular folk lectures and Bian Wen (a popular form of narrative literature) of the Tang Dynasty, and storytelling of the Song Dynasty, which can be further traced back to the performing arts in India and Central Asia.

Bianwen and other early Quyi rap were performed by looking at pictures and telling stories that were illustrated by these pictures. The American scholar Victor H. Mair's masterpiece *Paintings and Performances*, subtitled "*The Narration of Chinese Painting and Its Origin*", demonstrates by comparison the relationship between Bianwen and the "Look, Say and Perform" of ancient India, the Central and South Asia.

Surely, the influence of foreign arts on Chinese people is subtle and imperceptible. Most of the artists at the Majie Quyi Fair are not well educated and

的诗体是元曲，曲乐与词乐属于同一体系，它是在词乐基础上发展演化而来的。和唐诗、宋词一样，元曲是一种诗歌形式，但同时它也是一种戏剧。人们将若干支曲子按照一定规律串在一起，组成戏剧。从音乐上看，元曲分为北曲和南曲。前者使用七声音阶，以琵琶定调，节奏较快；后者使用五声音阶，以笛定调，节奏舒缓。在元代北曲要比南曲更为流行。

从金元时代开始流行的北曲使用河南方言，也就是"中州音韵"，或称"河洛正音"，来演唱。不仅语音是河南的，元曲的故事也是河南的。宋、金、元时代的戏曲，尤其是元代后期之前的戏曲，讲述的故事大多数发生在河南，特别是开封、洛阳和郑州三座城市。

4、丝绸之路与民俗曲艺

史书记载，李隆基退位以后，过着忧郁的闲居生活。为了替他排解忧愁，侍候他的宦官把市井之中各种曲艺表演者召进宫廷。

唐代是曲艺艺术发展成熟的关键时期，无论是魔术、杂技还是说唱故事，都已略具后世的雏形，这些艺术形式与印度、伊朗等地都有联系。沿丝绸之路进入中国的杂技幻人，屡见于中国史书的记载。在中国人看来，古罗马人有神奇的杂技艺术。河南新野出土的汉代画像砖上，有高鼻深目、戴尖顶帽的胡人口吐火焰的形象。据《魏略》记载，大秦国（古罗马）"俗多奇幻，口中出火，自缚自解，跳十二丸，巧妙非常"。此处所云吐火、跳丸、绳技是后来中国杂技最重要的几类。唐代来中国的印度艺人也以擅长幻戏之术著称，相关记载与罗马幻人非常接近。

河南省西南部，伏牛山脚下的宝丰县马街村，每年正月十三都有一场热闹的盛会。成千上万的曲艺艺人从全国各地汇集到这个不起眼的小村，在地上摆开简单的行头，表演自己的绝活。几十个曲艺品种争奇斗艳，最后由观众评出"书会状元"。这里往往能看到非常罕见、近乎失传的剧种。所有这些曲艺艺术，源头都可以追溯到唐代的俗讲、变文和宋代的说话。

might be unaware that their arts have exotic origins.

Both the form of performance and the content of the art of storytelling and singing in the Tang Dynasty had something to do with the Silk Road. In the early Tang Dynasty, Master Xuan Zang (also called Tang Monk, Tang Sanzang), also a cultural giant, was born in Yanshi County, Luoyang. The story of "Tang Monk's Pilgrimage to the West for the Buddhist Scriptures" is one of the most popular legendary stories in China. The early version of this story had been in existence during the late Tang Dynasty and the Five Dynasties, and was recorded in the *Poem on Sanzang Striven for Buddhist Scriptures in Great Tang Dynasty* in which there is no supernatural Monkey King, neither Guanyin Bodhisattva to save the suffering, instead, the figure who protected Tang Monk all the way to the west was Vaisramana. Belief in this deity dates back to some myths or legends of India. A lot of legendary stories, sculptures and paintings about Vaisramana can be found in the folk cultures of the Tang Dynasty. Several of his statues are found in Longmen Grottoes, Luoyang. For example, beside the statue of Locanabuddha in Fengxian Temple, stands in attendance the statue of Vaisramana in armour with calmness and might.

Quyi art performances are often associated with folk activities. In the Tang Dynasty, many customs of the Western Regions were accepted by the Chinese, and sports activities and music and dance performances were affected most. Polo, originated in Persia, was a kind of game played with the players on horseback hitting the ball. It was a very popular sport during the Tang Dynasty. The ball was made of light and tough wood with painted exterior, hard and smooth. In the competition, players on each side hit the ball with their polo stick (mallet) and tried to get it to the opponents' goal. The side that drove the ball more times to the opponent's goal won the game.

Polo had been introduced to Chang'an in the era of Emperor Taizong of the Tang Dynasty. In Chapter 6 of *The Sketch Book of Mr. Feng* by Feng Yan, it states, "Emperor Taizong often visited to Anfu Gate, and said, 'I heard that people from the Western Regions like to play polo, I watched once and I wanted our people to learn it. Yesterday, some foreigners played on the street nearby Shengxian Building and tried to attract me. This foreigner speculated that I loved the game and would try his best to play.'" This implies that those who often played this game in Chang'an at that time were mainly Hu people and this sport had aroused the interest of the

所有这些早期的曲艺形式，都可以追溯到印度和中亚的一些表演艺术。

变文等早期的曲艺说唱是配图的表演，对着图画讲述故事。美国学者梅维恒的名著《绘画与表演》，副标题是"中国绘画叙事及其起源研究"，他将变文与古代印度、中亚、南亚等地的看图讲故事表演相互比较，论证了它们之间的联系。

当然，外来曲艺艺术对中国人的影响是潜移默化的。马街书会上的艺人大多文化水平不高，并不知道他们的艺术有着异国渊源。

不只是演出形式，唐代说唱艺术的内容也和丝绸之路有关。唐初洛阳偃师曾诞生过一位文化巨人——玄奘法师。"唐僧取经"是中国人最喜爱的传统故事之一。这个故事的雏形在唐末五代时期已经出现，后载于《大唐三藏取经诗话》。不过在这本书里，还没有神通广大的孙大圣，也没有救苦救难的观音菩萨，保护唐僧取经的主要是毗沙门天王。毗沙门天王信仰的起源，与印度的一些神话传说有关。唐代民间通俗文化中，有很多关于毗沙门天王的故事传说、雕刻和绘画。在洛阳龙门石窟中就有多处毗沙门天王的造像，比如龙门石窟艺术的巅峰之作——奉先寺卢舍那大佛，旁边就有身着甲胄、沉着威武的天王像侍立。

曲艺演出往往与民俗活动有联系。在唐代，很多西域风俗被中国人接受，体育活动和乐舞表演受其影响最深。马球起源于波斯，是一种马上击球的游戏。马球是唐代非常流行的体育活动，球用质轻而有韧性的木料制成，外部彩绘，坚硬光滑。比赛时双方骑马争夺，用球杖击球，向对方进攻，击入多者胜。

马球运动在唐太宗时期已经传入长安。封演《封氏闻见记》卷六记载，"太宗常御安福门，谓侍臣曰：'闻西蕃人好为打球，比亦令习，会一度观之。昨升仙楼有群蕃街里打球，欲令朕见。此蕃疑朕爱此，骋为之。'"这反映出当时长安经常玩此游戏的主要是胡人，此运动也引起了唐太宗的兴趣。

洛阳也有文思球场，唐天祐元年（公元904年）七月，朱温自汴州

Emperor.

Luoyang also had a polo court called the Wensi Court. Zhu Wen (the first emperor of the Liang Dynasty in the period of the Five Dynasties) once came from Bianzhou (the present Kaifeng), and held a banquet there with all the central officials in lunar July of the 1st year of the Tianyou Era (904 A.D.). In the time of Emperor Zhongzong of the Tang Dynasty, Wu Chongxun, the Emperor's son in law, together with Yang Shenjiao built a polo court by spraying oil on the ground. It took millions of labors to build it, which seriously delayed the farm work, and caused great dissatisfaction. In Henan Province, where Luoyang is located, polo was also fashionable. Emperor Xuanzong of the Tang Dynasty built a court at his residence in Gaocheng County, Henan Province before he ascended to the throne. Chapter 19 of *Extensive Records of the Taiping Era* says, Chancellor Li Linfu "had not yet started schooling at the age of 20. He lived in the East Capital, and liked to hunt by chasing eagles and hounds, and play polo. He rode a donkey and played polo nearby the locust platform outside the city gate almost every single day". In the Kaicheng era of Emperor Wenzong of the Tang Dynasty (between 836 A.D. and 840 A.D.), "Many young ruffians in Henan, wearing high hats and bare-chested, played polo on official roads. No passengers dared to go past them." In 2003, a diamond-shaped bronze mirror was unearthed from a Tang Dynasty Tomb in Yichuan County, Luoyang. The ornamentation pattern on it is a scene of polo playing, with four players riding on horseback in various acts of swinging their polo sticks.

Bianzhou, like many other military towns, owned its own polo court. Zhu Youlun, a general from Bianzhou, played polo in Chang'an and died after falling off his horse in lunar September of the 3rd year of Tianfu Era (903 A.D.) of the Tang Dynasty. Many military officials were good at playing polo, such as Li Guangbi, who once played with an imperial envoy in Songzhou. Zhang Hu's poem, *Watching Tian Dafu Playing Polo in Songzhou*, described the scenes that he was watching when Tian Shengong was playing polo, "His white horse shook its red tassel when the ball was stroke and his purple sleeves waved." Obviously, polo was popular in the Yellow River Basin in the Tang Dynasty.

People in the Tang Dynasty developed a game, "Buda", on the basis of polo. In January, 2008, a tower shaped jar made of blue and white porcelain was unearthed in a Tang Dynasty tomb in Shangjie District, Zhengzhou. The picture on its body

至洛阳，与百官在文思球场饮宴。唐中宗时驸马武崇训、杨慎交洒油以筑球场，"用功数百万，妨害农务，敛怨于人"。洛阳所在的河南府击球之风亦盛，唐玄宗在藩邸时曾在河南府告成县辟有球场。《太平广记》卷十九还记载宰相李林甫"年二十，尚未读书。在东都，好游猎打球，驰逐鹰狗。每于城下槐坛下骑驴击鞠，略无休日"。唐文宗开成年间，"河南多恶少，或危帽散衣，击大球，户官道，车马不敢前"。2003 年，在洛阳伊川县唐墓中还曾出土过一件菱花形铜镜，其浮雕纹饰正是打马球的场景，四位球手骑乘骏马，手持鞠杖做出各种各样的姿态。

许多藩镇都设有球场，如汴州。唐天复三年（公元 903 年）九月，汴将朱友伦在长安击球坠马而亡。许多将领也善于打马球，如名将李光弼就曾在宋州与朝廷敕使打球。张祜《观宋州田大夫打球》就描述了在宋州观看田神功打马球时的场景，"白马顿红缨，梢球紫袖轻"。由此可见唐代黄河流域打马球风气之盛。

在外来马球的基础上，唐人还有所发明，出现了步打球。2008 年 1 月，在河南郑州上街区唐墓中出土了一件青花塔式罐，罐腹的图案上一人叉腿而立，右手扬弯形球杆，左侧有一圆球。考古工作者认为该图反映的就是唐代步打球的场景。

音乐民俗往往与外来民族的宗教活动有关。粟特人大多信奉祆教，在洛阳至少有四所祆祠，分别位于会节坊、立德坊、南市和西坊。粟特人能歌善舞，"每岁商胡祈福，烹猪羊，琵琶鼓笛，酣歌醉舞"。大量的西域胡人来到洛阳，还使泼寒胡戏也在洛阳流行。泼寒胡戏原本是康国的群众性歌舞活动。据《旧唐书》记载，"至十一月，鼓舞乞寒，以水相泼，盛为戏乐"。唐代流行的康国乐大约就是由此而来。《文献通考》中也有记载："乞寒，本西国外蕃康国之乐。其乐器有大鼓、小鼓、琵琶、五弦、箜篌、笛。其乐大抵以十一月，裸露形体，浇灌衢路，鼓舞跳跃而索寒也。"模仿胡人的舞蹈以及他们的生活习惯，唐人创作了《苏幕遮》《菩萨蛮》等舞曲。这些舞曲也是后来词乐的重要来源。

describes a person with his legs apart, waving a bow-shaped stick. On his left is a ball. Some archaeologists believe this picture depicts the scene of the Buda game of the Tang Dynasty.

Musical folklore of that time is often related to religious practices of foreign nationalities. Most Sogdian people believed in Zoroastrianism. Four Zoroastrianism temples in ancient Luoyang city were separately located at Huijie Fang, Lide Fang, the South Market and the West Fang. The Sogdian people were good at singing and dancing. "Every year, Hu businessmen celebrated prayer festivities by cooking and eating pork and veal, singing and dancing with the Pipa, drum and flute music." For example, Hu people pouring in from the Western Regions led to the popularity of the Water Spraying of the Hu people in Luoyang which was originally a folk dancing and singing activity in the Kang Kingdom (Samarkand, in Uzbekistan). *Old Book of Tang* recorded, "By the eleventh month, people dance to pray when the weather gets cold, playfully spraying water on one another. It is popular and entertaining." The Kang Music which was popular during the Tang Dynasty most probably originated from this practice. *Comprehensive Textual Research of the Historical Documents* also recorded, "The cold weather prayer was a tune from the Kang Kingdom. It involved in instruments of big drums, small drums, Pipa, Five-strings, Konghou and flutes to play. The tune described people half naked, spraying water on one another and dancing on the street to pray when cold days come." People of the Tang Dynasty created the dance music like *Sumuzhe, Pusaman* and so on by imitating their dancing and customs which later became the important sources of Ci music.

Silk Road, the old and yet modern term, reminds us of the smoke in desert, the sunset against long river, the ancient road and the twinkling sound of the camel ring. It is an important medium for ethnic integration and regional cooperation, and a transportation route with ancient Chinese stories. With the advent of the new era, we have given it a new historical mission, namely, to strengthen regional cooperation along the Silk Road, achieve mutual benefit and win-win, and build a community with a shared future for mankind. The old Silk Road has taken on new vitality.

Henan, located in the "center of the world", is an important transportation hub and plays an irreplaceable role in the history of the Silk Road. Here, the ancient culture never stops developing, religions are spreading, poetry vigorating, porcelain, tea, silk fabrics are being traded, medicine, astronomy are also constantly

丝绸之路，一个既古老又现代的名字。何谓古老，它会让我们想起大漠孤烟、长河落日，想起古道漫漫、驼铃悠悠，它是民族融合、域域合作的重要媒介，是诉说古老中国故事的交通线路。随着新时代的到来，我们又赋予它新的历史使命，即加强丝绸之路沿线区域合作，实现互利共赢，共建人类命运共同体。古老的丝绸之路焕发出新的生命力。

河南，地处"天下之中"，地理位置优越，是丝绸之路的重要交通枢纽，在丝绸之路发展史上发挥了不可替代的作用。在这里，古老的文化一直在流动，宗教在传播，诗歌在涌动，瓷器、茶叶、丝织品在穿梭，医药、天文学等也在不断地传播，这是穿越时空的交流、打破地域的对话。河南以其独特的区位与文化优势，成为东西方文化交流的桥头堡，扮演着重要角色。中原在崛起，河南在腾飞，我们要坚定文化自信，继续谱写丝绸之路新篇章。

communicated. Here people can sense the culture across time and space, and feel the the dialogue between different regions. Henan, with its unique location and cultural advantages, has been playing an important role in the cultural exchanges between the East and the West. We firmly believe that the ancient Silk Road is striding to a new era.

附录
Appendix

中国历史年代简表
A Brief Chronology of Chinese History

五帝时代 Period of the Five Legendary Rulers c. 2600 BC–c. 2070 BC	黄帝 Huangdi (Yellow Emperor)	
	颛顼 Zhuanxu	
	帝喾 Diku (Emperor Ku)	
	尧 Yao	
	舜 Shun	
夏 Xia Dynasty	c. 2070 BC–c. 1600 BC	
商 Shang Dynasty	c. 1600 BC–c. 1046 BC	
西周 Western Zhou Dynasty	c. 1046 BC–c. 771 BC	
东周 Eastern Zhou Dynasty 770 BC–256 BC	春秋 Spring and Autumn Period	770 BC–476 BC
	战国 Warring States Period	475 BC–221 BC
秦 Qin Dynasty	221 BC–206 BC	
汉 Han Dynasty 206 BC–220 AD	西汉 Western Han	206 BC–25 AD
	东汉 Eastern Han	25 AD–220 AD
三国 Three Kingdoms 220 AD–280 AD	魏 Wei	220 AD–265 AD
	蜀汉 Shu Han	221 AD–263 AD
	吴 Wu	222 AD–280 AD
晋 Jin Dynasty 265 AD–420 AD	西晋 Western Jin	265 AD–317 AD
	东晋 Eastern Jin	317 AD–420 AD

续表 Continued Table

南北朝 Southern and Northern Dynasties 420 AD-589 AD	南朝 Southern Dynasties	宋 Song	420 AD-479 AD
		齐 Qi	479 AD-502 AD
		梁 Liang	502 AD-557 AD
		陈 Chen	557 AD-589 AD
	北朝 Northern Dynasties	北魏 Northern Wei	386 AD-534 AD
		东魏 Eastern Wei	534 AD-550 AD
		北齐 Northern Qi	550 AD-577 AD
		西魏 Western Wei	535 AD-556 AD
		北周 Northern Zhou	557 AD-581 AD
隋 Sui Dynasty	581 AD-618 AD		
唐 Tang Dynasty	618 AD-907 AD		
五代十国 Five Dynasties and Ten States	五代 Five Dynasties 907 AD-960 AD	后梁 Later Liang	907 AD-923 AD
		后唐 Later Tang	923 AD-936 AD
		后晋 Later Jin	936 AD-947 AD
		后汉 Later Han	947 AD-950 AD
		后周 Later Zhou	951 AD-960 AD
	十国 Ten States 902 AD-979 AD	北汉 Northern Han	951 AD-979 AD
		吴 Wu	902 AD-937 AD
		吴越 Wuyue	907 AD-978 AD
		闽 Min	909 AD-945 AD
		南汉 Southern Han	917 AD-971 AD
		荆南（又称"南平"） Jingnan (Nanping)	924 AD-963 AD
		楚 Chu	927 AD-951 AD
		南唐 Southern Tang	937 AD-975 AD
		前蜀 Former Shu	907 AD-925 AD
		后蜀 Later Shu	934 AD-965 AD

续表 Continued Table

宋 Song Dynasty 960 AD-1279 AD	北宋 Northern Song	960 AD-1127 AD
	南宋 Southern Song	1127 AD-1279 AD
辽 Liao (契丹 Qidan/Khitan)	907 AD-1125 AD	
金 Jin	1115 AD-1234 AD	
西夏 Xixia (Tangut)	1038 AD-1227 AD	
元 Yuan Dynasty	1206 AD-1368 AD	
明 Ming Dynasty	1368 AD-1644 AD	
清 Qing Dynasty	1616 AD-1911 AD	
中华民国 Republic of China	1912 AD-1949 AD	
中华人民共和国 People's Republic of China	1949 AD-	